THE BIG SLEEP:
True Tales and Twisted Trivia
About Death

THE BIG SLEEP:
True Tales and Twisted Trivia About Death

Erica Orloff &
JoAnn Baker

SATURN PRESS

The Big Sleep: True Tales and Twisted Trivia about Death
Copyright © 1998 Erica Orloff and JoAnn Baker

Library of Congress Cataloging-in-Publication data.
ISBN: 1-885843-09-7
CIP: 98-06119

Printed in the United States of America 1 2 3 4 5 6 7 8 9 10

Cover design by Lightbourne Images, Inc.
Interior design by Pamela Morrell
Back cover photo by Angelina Collins

Published by:
Saturn Press, Inc.
17639 Foxborough Lane
Boca Raton, FL 33496

DEDICATION

*To all the dearly departed souls whose stories
never ceased to amaze us.*

ACKNOWLEDGMENTS

No book is the singular accomplishment of the author. We would like to thank Kathy and Marc Levinson at Saturn Press for their support and belief in this project, and their collective sense of humor.

Erica would like to thank the members of Writer's Cramp, Pam and Becky, for their encouragement and for putting up with her attacks on hyphens and commas. She would also like to thank Joyce and Marge, her e-mail pals, for reminding her to keep writing. She would like to express her gratitude to her father, Walter, for inspiring her to reach for the top; her mother, Maryanne, for instilling a love of reading that has helped her carve out a career for herself; her sisters, Jessica and Stacey, for being sisters and friends. Finally, she would like to express her deepest gratitude to her husband, John Diaz, for teaching her to laugh, and her children, Alexa, Nicholas, and Isabella, for their hugs and smiles.

JoAnn would like to thank the staff at the MF library, especially Marilyn McIntosh and Pauline Brower (sniff . . . sniff, I can't find anything since you left); Ed and Kath, who provided temporary office space (much roomier than the home office, I might add); Elizabeth Parsons for her support and Internet expertise; and, as always, my guys, Bob, Joe, and Chris.

PREFACE

Tick . . . Tick . . . Tick . . . It's only a matter of time. In the end, death is the great equalizer of mankind. We don't generally care to talk about it (especially in reference to ourselves), but it has always been a favorite topic for literature, art, movies, even sitcoms and jokes. So, why not a trivia book?

The Big Sleep: True Tales and Twisted Trivia about Death was written because of the subject's universal inevitability, and also because of the undeniable allure of the macabre.

When we began the book, we were normal. Well, sort of, anyway. But submerged in research on death, we each began to exhibit an obsessive interest in the subject. This has us a little concerned, because our next *True Tales and Twisted Trivia* book will be about sex. By that time, we will have completely lost the art of ordinary small talk.

In the meantime, using our newly collected information, we have managed to rivet, gross out, and amaze almost everyone we know. Now, it's your turn.

Erica Orloff
JoAnn Baker

TABLE OF CONTENTS

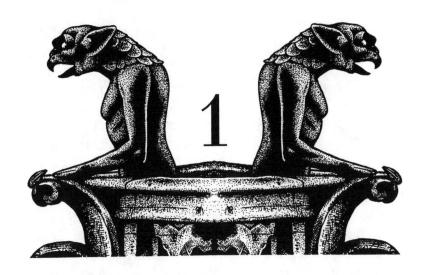

DYING TO BE RICH AND FAMOUS

"How were the circus receipts at Madison Square Garden tonight?"

P.T. Barnum, a businessman to the end

So, how do you want to go? In a blaze of glory? For most of us, death will come from heart disease or accident. If you're lucky, perhaps you will just go to sleep and not wake again. (Which, by the way, is the typical American's response to "How would you like to go?") If you're unlucky, perhaps you too could become fodder for our "What a Way to Go" chapter.

Last words of
Victor Hugo, said to be a
student of the occult:

"I see a black light."

You might think that the deaths of the rich and famous are somehow spectacular or romantic. However, because most of them still put on their pants one leg at a time (except Rin Tin Tin and Benji, who don't bother), celebrities and famous people die in boring or painful ways like the rest of us. Jimmy Stewart, John Wayne, Burgess Meredith, Gilda Radner, Groucho Marx, and countless others died after illness or infirmary, or simply of old age. George Burns made it to his 100th birthday before finally giving a command performance at that nightclub in the sky. But it *does* sometimes seem as if the famous go out in ways as fascinating as their lives.

ANTE UP

James Butler "Wild Bill" Hickock, left this world in a way destined to become part of folklore. Wild Bill always sat with his back to the wall. On the final day of his life, a friend jokingly took Wild Bill's usual seat and Wild Bill was left with his back to the door. While holding two pairs (aces and eights), he was shot through the head. Not surprisingly, aces and eights is known as the "dead man's hand" among avid poker players. Take a lesson. Always sit with your back to the wall.

Last words of
General Sedgewich during the Civil War at the Battle of Spotsylvania:

"They couldn't hit an elephant at this dist—..."

GOODBYE CRUEL WORLD

Some famous people long for the bright lights their whole lives, only to find that public adoration, wealth, and a household name are not enough to stave off loneliness, despair, and the feel of cold steel pressed against the temple or a large handful of pills sliding down the throat. While suicide is on the rise worldwide, the famous are no strangers to taking matters into their own hands.

Last words, scrawled in pen, of actor Richard Burton:

"Our revels are now ended."

Bruno Bettelheim was one of the greatest known American psychoanalysts of the 20th century. Considered a pioneer in the treatment of autistic children, Bettelheim nonetheless battled depression. He had spent time in a Nazi concentration camp and, later, his reputation was sullied when it was suggested that perhaps his "pioneering" treatments were not as humane as he had led the public to believe. Finally, the noted psychoanalyst swallowed an overdose of barbiturates, covered his head with a plastic bag, and killed himself. Physician . . . heal thyself.

Ernest Hemingway shot himself to escape his inner demons. Deeply depressed, Hemingway had tried electroshock therapy at the Mayo Clinic before he returned to his home and, ignoring his title *A Farewell to Arms*, used a shotgun to end his life. Family history was to repeat itself when granddaughter Margeaux Hemingway committed suicide many years later. (Her death was less violent—an overdose of pills.)

EUPHEMISMS

Taking the big dirt nap
Buying the farm
Becoming a landowner
Pushing up daisies
Biting the dust

Guns have often played a starring role in infamous sucides. Kurt Cobain and Freddie Prinz were both young and seemingly destined for long and rewarding careers. Prinz had starred on the popular 1970s "Chico and the Man" series with Jack Albertson. Rocker Cobain, lead singer of Nirvana, drew huge crowds of screaming fans and endless airplay on MTV. "Smells Like Teen Spirit" became an anthem for the slacker generation and the grunge culture movement of Seattle. He was married to fellow musician, Courtney Love, with whom he fathered a child. But a struggle with heroin and emotional problems took their toll on Cobain, and all the adoring fans in the world could not save him.

A sweets-lover to the end, the last words, spoken after he had a strawberry ice cream soda, of Lou Costello of Abbott and Costello fame:

"That was the best ice cream soda I ever tasted."

Sylvia Plath detailed all her torments in *The Bell Jar,* as well as in her poetry. She held the admiration of many young women of her generation who heard their own feminist voices in her words. Despite literary accolades, Plath remained despondent. Her husband left her for another woman. Depressed for much of her life, Plath eventually escaped by turning on a gas oven and shutting all the windows.

LIVE FAST, DIE YOUNG, LEAVE A PRETTY CORPSE

Sometimes suicide is passive. The person may not intend to die, but by the way he or she lives life in the fast lane, observers will comment it was only a matter of time. The recent drug-related death of comedic actor Chris Farley was just the latest in a long line of famous people whose wild ways contributed to their deaths. Other actors and actresses, writers and musicians whose deaths were attributed to alcohol or drugs include: John Belushi, who weighed 222 pounds when he died at age 33 from cocaine and heroin abuse; Jimi Hendrix, who died at the age of 27 after ingesting too many sleeping pills and choking on his own vomit; Billie Holiday, who died of heart failure at the age of 44 after a lifetime of heroin addiction; Janis Joplin, who died at age 27 after injecting herself with a large dose of very pure heroin; Elvis Presley, who technically died of a heart attack at age 42, though certainly the 10 different drugs found in his bloodstream did not help matters; and Jim Morrison (whose death was ruled a heart attack, but who had supposedly snorted heroin on the night of July 2, 1971). Morrison's gravesite in Paris is a popular tourist attraction, though French officials probably wish otherwise—it is a target for vandals and worshipping fans who leave debris, empty booze bottles, and graffitti on his tombstone.

And another erroneous statement—Last words of Terry Kath, a rock and roller, as he was playing Russian roulette:

"Don't worry, it's not loaded."

Gia, the model sensation of the flamboyant disco era, died of AIDS after a struggle with heroin. River Phoenix collapsed of drug use, a young and talented life cut short. But the long list of famous people who lived fast and died young didn't start with today's Hollywood and literary circles. As far back as 1916, writer Jack London died of an overdose of morphine at the age of 40. Artist Henri de Toulouse-Lautrec died in 1901, at the age of 37, after abusing his body for years through alcoholism compounded by syphilis.

Words on the flower arrangement Jackie Gleason sent to famed restaurateur Toots Shor's funeral:

"Save a table for me, pal."

Last words of
Karl Marx:

"Last words are for fools
who haven't said enough."

LONE GUNMEN AND OTHER FAIRY TALES (OR ELVIS AT THE CORNER 7-11)

Sometimes a famous person dies and a mystery still remains. An autopsy says one thing, but the public cannot accept the news. Or some believe a conspiracy is at work.

Elvis Presley died and his fans were anguished. When Pricilla Presley opened Graceland, his opulant home, to the public, Elvis adorers came by plane, bus, and automobile to pay homage to The King. But before Elvis's body had cooled, rumors spread that he was actually still alive. Fans cite his mispelled middle name on his grave marker at Graceland as proof. And then there are those sightings! Elvis has been spotted everywhere from the local 7-11 to ashrams in India. The simplest explaination? Why, all those Elvis impersonators, of course. They range from those who look like the young King, all the way up to heavyweights in tight-fitting, spangled jumpsuits and muttonchop sideburns who look like the Elvis of the last few years of his life—bloated and jewelry bedecked. There are flying Elvises in parachutes and Elvises (or is it "Elvi") who will croon to you in Vegas chapels. Or even perform the ceremony. And what about those people who speak to the spirit of Elvis? Their experiences were compiled in a book entitled: *Elvis After Life: Unusual Psychic Experiences Surrounding the Death of a Superstar*. The most logical conclusion to all this? Elvis was kidnapped by aliens with a penchant for "Blue Suede Shoes."

Marilyn Monroe died of an apparent accidental overdose in

Last words of
Somerset Maugham:

"Dying is a very dull, dreary affair and my advice is to have nothing whatever to do with it."

HOW OLD WOULD THEY BE TODAY?

	Age at Death	Birth Date	Death Date
1. John Belushi	33	1949	1982
2. Janis Joplin	27	1943	1970
3. Jimi Hendrix	28	1942	1970
4. Otis Redding	26	1941	1967
5. John Lennon	40	1940	1980
6. Elvis Presley	42	1935	1977
7. James Dean	24	1931	1955
8. Anne Frank	16	1929	1945
9. Martin Luther King, Jr.	39	1929	1968
10. Marilyn Monroe	36	1926	1962
11. Robert F. Kennedy	43	1925	1968
12. Malcolm X	40	1925	1965
13. Rocky Marciano	46	1923	1969
14. Judy Garland	47	1922	1969
15. John F. Kennedy	46	1917	1963
16. Christa McAuliffe	37	1949	1986
17. Jacqueline Kennedy Onassis	64	1929	1993
18. Princess Diana	36	1961	1997
19. Michael Landon	54	1937	1991
20. John Denver	53	1944	1997
21. Jacques Cousteau	87	1910	1997
22. Abbie Hoffman	53	1936	1989
23. Sergei Grinkov	28	1967	1995
24. Lucille Ball	78	1911	1989
25. Andy Warhol	58	1929	1987
26. Fred Astaire	88	1899	1987
27. Chris Farley	33	1964	1997
28. Jackie Gleason	71	1916	1987
29. Gene Kelly	84	1912	1991
30. Audrey Meadows	65	1926	1991
31. Sonny Bono	63	1935	1998
32. Jerry Garcia	53	1942	1995

Last words of
Voltaire when his bedside lamp flared:

"What? The flames already?"

her home . . . Or did she? Former lovers and those out for a buck have come forward with their theories on the "Marilyn Conspiracy." It is widely known she had an affair with John F. Kennedy. The conspiracy poses the idea that JFK and his brother Robert plotted to kill her in order to keep the unstable Marilyn from making her presidential affair public. Then, as the theory goes, Peter Lawford or the FBI . . . or both . . . found her diary and stole it from her home to ensure the "secret" affair would die with Marilyn, a.k.a. Norma Jean. According to these conspiracy theorists, Marilyn didn't die from an overdose. Instead, a tiny puncture mark was missed by the coroner and she was injected with some substance that caused her early demise.

Perhaps, we don't want to allow some of our most beloved figures to die. Or we can't believe they could go in such an ordinary or careless way. More recently, Princess Diana got into a car with a drunk driver. But rather than accepting her death from this tragic crash, a mysterious Fiat entered the picture as the French police scoured the country for the vehicle that may have caused the accident. Britain's florists eventually had to stop taking flower orders because the demand was so great after her death, and the public turned out in record numbers to show their grief.

In the case of John F. Kennedy, we even have film of his assassination but this has not quelled the speculation. Slowing the assassination footage down, experts have watched which way the president's body jerked in reaction to the shots. Was there a second shooter on the grassy knoll? Oliver Stone's movie, *JFK*, took conspiracy theory to its highest level, posing Stone's version of what may have happened to America's late president—complete with mysterious informants and covert meetings.

LOSING ONE'S HEAD

You've heard of keeping your wit's about you. Try keeping your head. Saint Sir Thomas More resigned from his post as Lord Chancellor of England when Henry VIII demanded a divorce from Catherine of Aragon. More, for his protests, was imprisoned in the Tower of London, and after a futile trial whose outcome was determined before it even started, he was sentenced to be executed. As was the custom, he was beheaded. And, lest anyone think that punishment was not enough of a deterrent, his head was parboiled (Is there a recipe for this? Just how long does one parboil a human head?) and stuck on a stake above London Bridge. (Funny, why didn't they include this story in the children's verse?)

Of course, other famous folks have lost their heads. Jayne Mansfield was decapitated during a car accident in which her vehicle collided with a massive truck. And Isadora Duncan was nearly beheaded after her flowing scarf caught beneath the wheel of the car in which she was riding. Killed by fashion, perhaps Isadora would advise today's youth to pull up those baggy pants.

Final words of
George Eastman (man who started the Kodak Company) prior to his suicide by gunshot:

"To my friends, my work is done. Why wait?"

EVEN A TOMBSTONE CAN'T KEEP US APART

Comedian Jack Benny was greatly loved by legions of fans. Despite an onscreen persona of cheapness (and that horrible violin playing), he was a generous man, particularly with his wife, the actress Mary Livingstone.

Last words of
Lytton Stachey, a critic:

"If this is dying, I don't think much of it."

Prior to his death, he told his florist to "send my doll a red rose every day." Benny's will stipulated that funds were to be set aside to deliver to Mary Livingstone a single long-stemmed red rose every day for the rest of her life.

Another Hollywood husband—who took his devotion a step further—was Charles Boyer, one of film's great screen lovers. But it was his real-life marriage to Pat Paterson that made for the greatest love story of devotion and adoration. After 44 happy years of marriage, Pat Paterson died of cancer with her husband by her side in their Arizona home. All through her illness, Boyer cared for her and nursed her. Two days after her death, after methodically putting their affairs in order, Charles Boyer committed suicide, unable to live without his English-born actress-wife and confidant. The two are buried side by side in Holy Cross Cemetery in Los Angeles.

Last words of Oscar Wilde:

"My wallpaper and I are fighting a duel to the death. One or the other of us has to go."

NO ACCOLADES, PLEASE

When Al Jolson died, he made provisions for a massive monument and large funeral service to commemorate the occasion. But not everyone longs for a public display. Golda Meir was Israel's prime minister from 1969 to 1974. She was known as a no-nonsense, strong-willed woman. She had to be, ruling a country surrounded by unfriendly territory and internally divided by politics. Prior to her death, she specified that she wanted no eulogies spoken after her death and she wanted "nothing named for me." In Israel, to this day, no buildings, highways, or public works are named for the respected woman.

FAMOUS PEOPLE WHO DIED OF AIDS

1. Peter Allen	age 48	1944–1992	entertainer/songwriter
2. Arthur Ashe	age 50	1943–1993	tennis player
3. Amanda Blake	age 60	1929–1989	actress
4. Roy Cohn	age 59	1927–1986	lawyer
5. Brad Davis	age 42	1949–1991	actor
6. Perry Ellis	age 46	1940–1986	fashion designer
7. Halston	age 58	1932–1990	fashion designer
8. John C. Holmes	age 43	1945–1988	porn star
9. Rock Hudson	age 60	1925–1985	actor
10. Liberace	age 68	1919–1987	entertainer/pianist
11. Robert Mapplethorpe	age 43	1946–1989	photographer
12. Freddy Mercury	age 45	1946–1991	rock singer—Queen
13. Rudolf Nureyev	age 55	1938–1993	ballet dancer
14. Anthony Perkins	age 60	1932–1992	actor
15. Robert Reed	age 60	1932–1992	actor

FAMOUS FOR ALL THE WRONG REASONS

We all know about the deaths of Sonny Bono, Mother Teresa, and Princess Diana. Their deaths stayed in the news from the "funeral watch," to funeral coverage, to endless media reports and editorials about their contributions to the world. But there are other people who lived relatively quiet lives and achieved infamy because of the circumstances surrounding their deaths.

Such is the story of Casey Jones, an everyday sort of railroad man who was immortalized in song and legend because of his heroic last moments. He saved countless lives when he realized the train he was driving was heading for a collision. After telling his coworkers to jump, he died with one hand on the brake and the other on the whistle.

Nathan Hale earned a place in American history when he was hung as a spy. Ironically, the thing for which he was most famous—his last words—is a misquote. ("I regret that I have but one life to give to my country.")

Mary Jo Kopechne, previously known to only family and friends, became a household name when she died in Senator Edward Kennedy's car under questionable circumstances. Kennedy drove his car off a bridge in Chappaquiddick (a small town whose name also exploded off the map) and left the scene—leaving Kopechne's drowned body in the backseat. Questions as to Kennedy's sobriety and whether he and the young political worker were having an affair have never been answered.

Leo and Rosemary LaBianca became famous for all the wrong reasons when they were brutally murdered by members of the Manson "family" cult. Sharon Tate, a young actress and wife of director Roman Polanski, and her unborn baby were also slaughtered. The incident became known as the Tate-LaBianca murders.

Henrietta Lacks's name may be unknown to most—but she is famous worldwide in medical circles. Lacks died in 1951 of cervical cancer, but her cancer cells were so extraordinarily prolific that they have been bred and used in research ever since. First identified at Johns Hopkins University in Baltimore, the cells are now used all over the globe. They are referred to as HeLa cells.

TOUCHE!

And a final word of insult. . . . William Gladstone was the political enemy of Benjamin Disraeli, the prime minister of England during the the reign of Queen Victoria. Gladstone said, publicly, that Disraeli would "die by the hangman's noose or a vile disease." To which Disraeli replied, "Sir, that depends upon whether I embrace your principles or your mistress."

POP QUIZ

QUESTIONS (Answers start on page 19.)

1. After a lifetime of adventure in the Old West, how did Wyatt Earp finally die?
   A. He was shot in the back by a cowardly enemy.
   B. He was shot in the back by a jealous lover.
   C. He died of cancer.
   D. He died "with his pants down," so to speak, with a local prostitute.

2. The world's most famous escape artist, how did Harry Houdini die?
   A. He drowned during his famous Chinese Water Torture trick.
   B. He committed suicide after his beloved mother died.
   C. He died of a blow to the stomach.
   D. His death, under mysterious circumstances, was never solved.

3. Zelda Fitzgerald, wife of F. Scott Fitzgerald, and a legendary beauty of the Jazz Age died:
   A. After being shot to death by Fitzgerald when he caught her in bed with a younger man.
   B. Of liver disease after a lifetime of partying and wild ways.

C. In a fire.

D. Of the ravages of syphilis.

4. Vincent Van Gogh lived to see only one painting—The Red Vine—sold. He died at age 37 from:

A. Complications from an infection after he cut off part of his left ear.

B. Suicide. He shot himself in the stomach.

C. Syphilis. He was known to have an affection for the prostitutes of the town of Arles in the south of France.

D. Starvation. Because he couldn't sell his paintings, he often went days and weeks without a nutritional meal.

5. Hans Christian Andersen, writer of "The Little Mermaid," "The Ugly Duckling," and "The Princess and the Pea" (among other stories), died at the age of 70. Notedly, he:

A. Was obsessed with his own death and slept in a coffin until his dying day.

B. Was a virgin at the time of his death.

C, Was actually a woman.

D. Asked to be buried at sea because he truly believed in mermaids.

6. The Marquis de Sade died:

A. After being injured during a violent sexual encounter with a dominatrix.

B. In an insane asylum.

C. During a duel with a jealous husband outraged by his affair with the man's wife.

D. Of a combination of sexually transmitted diseases.

7. How did Cleopatra (69–30 B.C.) die?

A. She committed suicide.

B. During childbirth.

C. After eating a poisoned apple, which is the root of the Snow White fairytale.

D. During a plague, supposedly one of Moses's as described in the Bible.

8. Aimee Semple McPherson was a big-money evangelist in the early 20th century. Famous as "Sister Aimee," she died:

A. Of an accidental drug overdose.

B. Of a botched abortion.

C. A suicide.

D. During childbirth.

9. Grigori Rasputin, the charismatic adviser to Czar Nicholas of Russia, died:

A. After being attacked by an unruly mob during the Russian Revolution.

B. After the Czarina shot him in a jealous rage when he threatened to end their decade-long affair.

C. After eating a bowl of spoiled borscht.

D. During an assassination masterminded by a group of noblemen.

10. Sigmund Freud, the father of psychoanalysis—the "talking cure"—died in 1939:

A. Of a self-inflicted gunshot wound, after he had grown despondent over the failure of his final book to garner critical praise.

B. Of a cocaine overdose.

C. When one of his patients, a repressed woman named "Martha B.," stabbed him during an emotional psychoanalytic session.

D. Of cancer of the jaw.

11. Clark Gable, the gallant actor who protrayed Rhett Butler, was said to have tried to save Jean Harlow's life. Harlow, the beautiful blond bombshell, died anyway. What were the circumstances surrounding her death?

    A. She died of a botched abortion performed after the first trimester.

    B. She died of alcohol poisoning after a night drinking with Gable on the set of their movie, *Red Dust*.

    C. She died of uremic posioning for which she had not sought medical attention.

    D. She committed suicide, shooting herself despite Gable's attempt to talk her out of it.

12. What were the circumstances of alleged spy Mata Hari's death?

    A. While performing on stage in the nude, she was killed by a crazed, lovesick fan.

    B. She died of old age, but in her declining years was said to be mad, wandering the streets of France as a vagrant.

    C. She was shot by a French firing squad.

    D. She was shot down in a plane over the Atlantic during WWI and her body was never recovered.

13. How did legendary Russian-American choreographer George Balanchine die?

    A. Of a form of Mad Cow Disease.

    B. Of complications following surgery on a tendon injured through years of punishing dance routines.

    C. He drowned during his daily four-mile ocean swim.

    D. From injuries sustained when he fell off stage during his last public performance.

14. Lizzie Bordon supposedly took an axe and gave her parents those fatal whacks years ago (a crime she was acquitted of). Of what did ol' Lizzie die?

    A. Old age.

    B. Suicide, leaving a note in which she finally confessed she had killed her parents in a "rage over which I had no control, Heaven forgive me."

    C. She was murdered, and the case was never solved, though it is alleged that the *real* killer of her parents returned to finish the job he had started twenty years before.

    D. No one knows. She disappeared from her hometown after her acquittal and was never heard from again.

15. Al "Scarface" Capone, the Chicago mobster, died in 1947 after a colorful life, including 10 years in prison for federal income tax evasion. How did he die?

    A. He was assassinated by rival mobsters while dining in his favorite Chicago eatery on his favorite meal, spaghetti Bolognese.

    B. He died while in prison after a bloody fight in the prison yard. Because other prisoners surrounded the combatants, blocking the view of the prison guards, the real killer of Scarface remains unknown to this day.

    C. He died of complications from syphilis.

    D. He died of old age, a grandfather of 12. It is said in his final years, Scarface, once the most feared man in Chicago, liked to have tea parties with his youngest grandchild, Alberta, named after her famous grandfather.

16. *Butch Cassidy and the Sundance Kid* imortalized two outlaws on celluloid. It depicted a final shootout in Bolivia, from which Butch Cassidy and the Kid could not

possibly have survived. Legend or fact? How did Butch Cassidy die?

A. Exactly as it was portrayed in the movie—minus the soundtrack and the gorgeous good looks of Paul Newman and Robert Redford.

B. Of cancer.

C. He was cornered in Boliva, but he was captured and then slowly tortured to death by a sadistic Bolivian soldier. The producers of the movie felt this would be too much of a downer for American film audiences so they re-wrote history for the sake of the film.

D. He was shot by the jealous husband of yet another female conquest.

17. Tennessee Williams, the famous American playwright, died in 1983. How did he die?

A. He died of a self-inflicted gunshot wound.

B. He choked to death.

C. He was struck by a cab while crossing the street in the Broadway theater district in New York City.

D. He died of AIDS before the disease leapt to the front pages of the media.

18. What was the controversy after the Duke of Windsor's death in 1972?

A. Queen Elizabeth, who owed her crown to his abdication, refused to attend his funeral.

B. One of England's "scandal rags" (tabloids) published accounts of his sexual exploits.

C. Wallis Simpson, the Duchess of Windsor, refused to greet Queen Elizabeth because the Queen had snubbed her throughout her marriage and had never given her the title of "Her Royal Highness."

D. His entire estate was left to his wife.

ANSWERS

1. C. He died of cancer.

2. C. He died of a blow to the stomach.

   Houdini died of peritonitis after receiving a blow administered by a fan. Houdini was famous for being able to take severe blows to the stomach—a "trick" he managed by preparing himself and tightening his stomach muscles rock solid. A student approached him and struck a blow before Houdini could ready himself and he died within days.

3. C. In a fire.

   Sadly, Zelda suffered several nervous breakdowns in her life. She was plagued by guilt over three abortions she had during her marriage to F. Scott, and she and the famous writer had an obsessive and tormenting relationship with one another. She burned to death during a fire in an insane asylum where she was confined.

4. B. Suicide.

   Poor Van Gogh is another famous person said to suffer from recurrent bouts of insanity. He spent a year in an asylum combatting madness. Ultimately, he shot himself in the stomach.

5. B. Was a virgin at the time of his death.

   Andersen was, interestingly, extremely phobic as well. He was terrified of fire and also of being buried alive. He made friends promise to slit one of his arteries before his burial in order to ensure that he was truly dead. So, while obsessed with death, he would *never* have slept in his own coffin. He died of cancer of the liver.

6. B. In an insane asylum.

   Sade (from whose name we have the word *sadism*) seemed to know no bounds when it came to his sexual exploits. Not only did he fervently enjoy inflicting and receiving pain during sexual encounters, he often recruited young prostitutes for orgies—sometimes causing them such injury they required medical attention. He was imprisoned after several prostitutes accused him of trying to poison them. Ultimately, he was confined to an asylum for the criminally insane, where he eventually died of natural causes in old age. However, even in the asylum, he was said to have enjoyed the services of a young laundry-worker on the asylum's staff.

7. A. She committed suicide.

    Cleopatra was a noted seductress. But when she needed her seduction powers the most, they failed her. She was captured by the enemy forces of Octavian after Mark Antony died in her arms (he stabbed himself to death after hearing a false report that she had died). She tried to use her sexual wiles to free herself, but to no avail. After hearing that she was to be humilated in the streets of Rome, Cleopatra killed herself.

8. A. Of an accidental drug overdose.

    Jim and Tammy Faye and the other fallen evangelists of modern times have nothing on Aimee McPherson. She had three failed marriages (despite tenets of her church forbidding remarriage while an ex-spouse was still living) and numerous affairs, allegedly including one with a then little-known comic named Milton Berle. She engineered a fake "kidnapping" of herself in 1926 in order to enjoy an illicit getaway with a married man. Inuendo followed her throughout much of her career, and she finally died of a barbiturate overdose in California.

9. D. During an assassination masterminded by a group of noblemen.

Rasputin was assassinated in 1916 after drinking poisoned wine and then being shot and beaten. But that's not all! The assassins also severed his penis (perhaps Lorena Bobbitt took a lesson here), allegedly a 13-inch organ that was preserved at least until 1968. *Still* not dead, he was tied up and thrown into the Neva River where he finally drowned.

10. D. Of cancer of the jaw.

    Ironically, the man who advocated the talking cure succombed to cancer of the palate and jaw. He smoked as many as 20 cigars a day—even after he was diagnosed with cancer. An advocate of assisted suicide, he asked a friend-physician to administer higher than normal levels of painkillers in the last days of his life to hasten death.

11. C. She died of uremic poisoning for which she had not sought medical attention.

    Harlow's second husband, Paul Bern, had an underdeveloped penis (said to be the size of an infant boy's), and he was completely impotent. He eventually shot himself in the head over his own frustration with being unable to consummate his marriage to Harlow. However, prior to his suicide, he had a reputation as a wife-beater and Harlow suffered from kidney problems because of a severe beating she allegedly received across her back with a cane. Eventually, the kidney problems caused uremic poisoning. However, Harlow's overbearing mother was a Christian Scientist who refused to allow her daughter to receive medical treatment. Before she died, Gable and various influential studio people tried to talk Harlow's mother into allowing them to obtain medical care for the ailing star. The mother refused and when she finally relented, it was too late. Harlow was 26 at the time of her death.

12. C. She was shot by a French firing squad.

   Mata Hari even requested that she not be blindfolded. No one ever claimed her body, and it was donated to a medical school for dissection. Mata Hari led a colorful life, to be sure. She danced naked on stage in her persona of an Indian temple dancer. She accepted money for sex and did sleep with a wealthy German in Berlin. However, scholars today say the evidence against her as an actual spy was scant. She was perhaps shot as much for rumor as for anything they could uncover proving her guilt.

13. A. Of a form of Mad Cow Disease.

   Balanchine died of Creutzfeldt-Jakob Syndrome, a form of the recently named "Mad Cow Disease," made famous by the beef scare in Great Britain. At the time of Balanchine's death in April of 1983, the syndrome was virtually unheard of. How did Balanchine contract it? Some hypothesize that animal extract injections that he took for their supposed rejuvenating properties infected him.

14. A. Old age.

   After her celebrated trial, Lizzie lived a quiet, stately life with the money from her inheritance. Was she guilty? Scholars now think she was. Apparently, certain bits of evidence were suppressed. Despite what the townsfolk may have thought, Lizzie had the last laugh, living in luxury until age 67.

15. C. He died of complications from syphilis.

   The neurosyphilis caused extensive brain damage and his last years in Florida were marked by obesity and insanity, though no offical autopsy showed the exact cause of death.

16. B. Of cancer.

    In the book *In Search of Butch Cassidy*, the author
    found Cassidy's sister who revealed Cassidy had re-
    turned to the United States and lived a respectable life
    in Washington, near Spokane. He died of rectal cancer
    in 1937.

17. B. He choked to death.

    Williams actually choked on the cap of a perscription
    bottle of eyedrops. He was, in his last years especially, a
    habitual pill taker and also drank large quantities of
    alcohol. Presumably in an impaired state, he put the cap
    in his mouth, apparently mistaking it for another pill. He
    choked to death in his Manhattan hotel suite.

18. D. His entire estate was left to his wife.

    Lord Mountbatten and others tried to have the Windsors'
    estate returned to Britain. Perhaps the Duke's decision
    to abdicate still rankled. But he had left his entire estate
    to his wife, Wallis. When she died, the estate again
    slipped through Britain's grasp, because she left the
    estate to the Pasteur Institute in Paris.

THE CULTURE OF DEATH

"You can be a king or a street sweeper, but everyone dances with the Grim Reaper."

—*Robert Alton Harris, before his 1992 execution*

Many Americans will die in hospitals, nursing homes, or hospices. As a country, we seem increasingly uncomfortable with death, preferring to keep it behind hospital curtains or at a safe distance. But in America's earlier history, death often occurred at home, with loved ones gathered around. The dead were laid out on boards right in the family parlor, and death was seen as part of the cycle of life, not a dreaded enemy.

Elsewhere around the globe, death has many different roles and the attitudes towards it vary. Here are some cultural holidays,

---

EUPHEMISMS

Being put to bed with a shovel
Snuffed out
The long goodbye
The big sleep
Bite the big one

---

days of the dead, and unusual death customs from other cultures and throughout history.

- ❧ Days of the Dead. Mexico's Days of the Dead are an annual "reunion" with loved ones who have passed to the Great Beyond. The days include edible baked "skulls" from local bakeries (called "bread of the dead"—how appetizing), bones made from marzipan, and other light-hearted and colorful aspects of a holiday. The family shrine is usually decorated with pictures of the deceased as well as artwork depicting saints. Celebrated on All Saints Day and All Souls Day (November 1 and 2).

- ❧ Feast of Hungry Ghosts. In China, this feast day was forbidden during the communist regime of Mao Tse-Tung and Chou-En-Lai as it celebrated spirit or soul. Interestingly, China also had a long tradition of ground burial, but during the revolution, this was frowned on as well. Cremation was encouraged by the Chinese government and hundreds of crematoriums were built. However, human nature is that people give up their burial customs reluctantly, and China's citizens rejected the idea of cremation. So the government then began offering the cremations at bargain basement prices. Buy one, get one free!

✦ Shunamatism. This term refers to the replenishing of life forces. In medieval Europe, it was believed that an old person who slept between two young people could receive a sort of transfusion of life force. People also ate "hot" and spicy foods with the same belief. As Roger Bacon was quoted: "If disease is contagious, why not vitality."

WATCH WHERE YOU SIT

The Ashantis of Ghana, Togo, and Cote d'Ivoire believed in the power of the stool. Each tribe has a golden stool—but no one is allowed to sit on it. Instead, ornaments and trophies of the tribe are mounted on it. Not even the Ashanti king can sit on the golden stool.

During funerals of dignitaries, a wooden stool is carved. The corpse is bathed and then the dead body is sat on the stool. Later, the stool is painted black in the presence of the golden stool and then the black stool is brought to the House of the Throne Stool where it is kept with the stools of other important people.

BUS FARE, ANYONE?

According to newspaper reports, Heaven's Gate cult members, who committed suicide en masse, each had money in their pockets, perhaps in some belief that they would either need money when they got to the other side of the Hale-Bopp comet or that the aliens arriving to take them on

Last words of World heavyweight boxing champ Max Baer, in a simple, straightforward punch:

"Oh, God, here I go!"

A cranky old man to the end, the final words of W. C. Fields, who died in 1946:

"Goddamn the whole friggin' world and everyone in it but you, Carlotta."

their cosmic journey would require American coinage as interplanetary bus fare—though if they have the technology to beam up passengers, why they would need American dollars is anyone's guess. However, this is not the first time that belief in a "death fare" made an appearance.

In Madagascar's cult of the dead, after death a coin is placed on the dead person's forehead. It represents the soul's fare and money for passage from this world to the next.

WHICH WAY DID THEY GO?

In the highlands of Madagascar, the dead are reburied during the cool season. But the reburial is not simply a matter of digging up a rotting corpse and moving it. Instead, the corpse is carried on a very circuitous route. Marched by family members through the hills, round and round, down unusual paths meant to confuse, the body is finally laid to rest in the family's ancestral home burial ground. Why the convoluted path? The idea is to confuse the spirit

---

EUPHEMISMS

Six feet under
Passed away
Passed on
Checked out
Curtains

so it does not follow the family members back to the village but instead remains in the ancestral home where it belongs.

MUMMY DEAREST

Egyptians usually buried their dead with valuables they might need in the next world. This might include servants who were thereby condemned to die in the mummy's tomb or pyramid in final service to their master. And they say you can't find good help.

Preparation of a mummy involved removing the brain and intestines. Next, linen mixed with a preservative of sodium, spices, and oils was inserted into the body. Next, this same mixture was applied to the outside of the body and then the entire body was wrapped in linen. The internal organs were kept in four separate urns, though the heart remained inside the mummy because even during ancient times, the heart was seen as a person's spiritual center.

Samuel Goldwyn, king of the malaprops:

"If Roosevelt were alive today, he would turn over in his grave."

For the poor, mummification was not an option and they were buried in shallow graves. The rich were not only mummified, they had monetary trusts to ensure that even after they were gone, priests of generations to come would continue to care for their tomb.

Pyramids were constructed as early as 2700 B.C. Within these immense tombs were painted scenes of the afterlife. Curses were also written into the hieroglyphics. If a tomb was disturbed by graverobbers (and later by archeologists), the spirit of the deceased was released to curse those who dared bother it. Alternately, the mummy's spirit could be lost entirely during

"I stayed up all night playing poker with tarot cards. I got a full house and four people died."

—Comedian Steven Wright

the break-in, thus Egyptians took the threat of grave robbery very seriously.

HOW MUCH WOULD THIS STAMP COST?

Ancient Egyptians also wrote letters to their dead. If someone died after an argument, oftentimes the survivors wrote remorseful letters in fear that, if not forgiven, the person might come back to exact vengeance.

However, Egyptians appear also to have written simply to continue their intimate relationships. The so-called "dead letters" found by archeologists sometimes are chatty notes about the day-to-day events of family members. Like humans throughout time, the Egyptians seemed to have wanted their relationships with the deceased to bridge that gap between living and dead.

A ROOM WITH NO VIEW

The Yombe of Zambia take the idea of an ancestral home literally. After a person dies, elaborate ceremonies are performed to maintain ties to the deceased who become part of their ancestral cult. When the grave is dug, it even includes a bedroom and a bed. How's that for real estate? When the dead body is placed in the grave, its eyes are positioned to "look" towards the mythical origins of the tribe.

Last words of John Barrymore

"Die? I should say not, dear fellow. No Barrymore would allow such a conventional thing to happen to him."

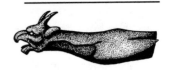

Later, a second burial ritual is performed that ends the mourning period. At the conclusion of this burial, an elder of the tribe transfers the spirit of the deceased to an object such as a hoe or tool. So Grandma Minnie just may be taking up residence in Dad's toolbox.

PAY THE MAN!

In Ghana, a tribe known as the LoGagaa believe when you die you have to pay a fee to a ferryman who will transport you to the land of the afterlife. The ferryman acts as a threshold guardian of the afterlife—a St. Peter on a boat.

Last words of Humphrey Bogart

"I should never have switched from Scotch to Martinis."

Like many religions with water symbolism, crossing the spiritual river brings you to everlasting life. However, in this particular tribe, you better not owe any debts prior to your death. Overdue bills mean you cannot cross the river until your creditor dies also, at which time you can pay the man and cross over to the other side.

The LoGagaa also have water symbolism in their version of heavenly comeuppance. If you led an evil life, you have to swim, ever-exhausted, for three years until you finally make it to the banks of heaven. Doggy paddle, anyone?

EAST, WEST, NORTH, OR SOUTH?

Aztec society, known for its human sacrifices, made distinctions of which direction you traveled after death depending on how you died. Human sacrifices went east to paradise and got to enjoy the sun. Seems a high price to pay for a tan. Human sacrifices were joined by warriors who died in battle and tradesmen who died during a journey. All three types of deceased people were cremated.

If you happened to drown, get struck by lightening, or suffer from marsh fever, you were buried underground and traveled south after death to a lucious garden.

Mothers who died during childbirth also got to enjoy the sun—but they went west, to the land of the setting sun.

Unfortunately, for the rest of Aztec society, the treacherous journey to the north was distinctly unpleasant—battling beasts, cold, winds, mountains, and a decidedly long and arduous trip to the land of the dead. Luckily, these hapless souls were buried with cremated dog remains that would help them along the way.

POP QUIZ

QUESTIONS (Answers start on page 36.)

1. Ch'in Shih-huan ti was the first emperor of United China. He was the leader who initiated the Great Wall. When he died, what was he buried with?

   A. His concubines.

   B. An entire life-size terra cotta army.

   C. The head of his brother, a lifelong enemy of the emperor who had been jealous of his power.

   D. Chopsticks.

2. How many men typically worked on Khufu's pyramid at one time?

   A. About 40,000.

   B. About 20,000.

   C. 6,666, a precise number which still confounds archeologists today.

   D. No one knows. No human remains were ever found there, leading to the infamous "alien" theory that perhaps UFOs and aliens landed and helped construct the pyramid with as yet undiscovered technology.

3. What have archeologists discovered from the tombs of workers who died while building the pyramids?

   A. They were all under 5'4" tall.

   B. Many of them appear to boys under the age of six.

C. They suffered from spinal and coccyx injuries and pathologies.

D. Their DNA contains elements scientists cannot explain yet.

4. In ancient Chinese history, what was the role of the mythical Queen Mother of the West?

A. She doled out drugs.

B. She helped the dead make contact with the living.

C. She gathered all the souls in a giant urn.

D. She was the spiritual wife of Confucious.

5. What is a meat body?

A. Smoked Buddhist monk.

B. The spirit of an animal that was killed while on earth and eaten as meat.

C. A large sausage from Germany with the power to prolong life.

D. Fried warthog, which to certain African tribes was a sacred funeral meal.

6. According to Egyptian legend, what unbelievable feat was Isis able to perform after the death of her husband, Osiris (who, incidentally, was also her brother)?

A. She was able to see into the future, using his eyeballs, which she refused to bury with the body.

B. After Osiris was dismembered by his enemy, she was able to piece him back together and become impregnated by him.

C. She was able to heal anyone by calling upon his spirit.

D. She was able to eat inordinate amounts of chocolate without gaining any weight.

7. What is the Hall of Justice, according to the ancient Egyptians?

   A. A place where all the superheros, including Superman, meet to plan their crimefighting tactics.

   B. An ancient temple where death sentences were carried out against infidels.

   C. A tomb where Ra, the sun-god, is supposedly buried.

   D. A place where, using the Book of the Dead, the deceased must account for their lives.

8. What is a Ghost Dance?

   A. Something one of the authors' great-uncles does after drinking too much wine at family weddings.

   B. A dance performed in honor of the Pharoahs.

   C. A dance performed by Native Americans to evoke the dead.

   D. It is not a dance at all, but refers to the way ghosts appear to shimmer and move subtly when they appear to humans.

9. According to ancient Mesopotamians, who or what was Ishtar?

   A. The ruler of the underworld.

   B. A bad Dustin Hoffman-Warren Beatty movie.

   C. The blessing people said to ward off soul-stealing beasts after someone sneezed.

   D. The name of the wise man who wrote that culture's Book of the Dead.

10. According to Zoroastrianism, a religion with origins in ancient Persia, what happens to the soul immediately after death?

A. It joins with other life forces in the good vs. evil battle—which side it goes to depends on the life of the deceased.

B. It attempts to enter into another's body, so people did not speak, eat, or open their mouths around the deceased person's body for one full night after death.

C. It collects at the head of the person and remains there for three days awaiting judgment.

D. It escapes into a pregnant woman or young mother in the community to be passed, through birth or through mother's milk, into a young baby's body.

ANSWERS

1. B. An entire life-size terra cotta army.

2. B. About 20,000.

   This is guessed to be the number of men working on Khufu's pyramid at any one time. The teams would work for three or four months, to be rotated with other teams of 20,000. The men in general worked nine days straight with one day off.

3. C. They suffered from spinal and coccyx injuries and pathologies.

   This is presumed to be from the excessive strain they experienced as they hauled and carried heavy stone during the building.

4. A. She doled out drugs.

   According to mythic history, the Queen Mother of the West doled out a drug with the power to make the deceased immortal. Those given the drug during funeral rites went directly to heaven.

5. A. Smoked Buddhist monk.

   Believe it or not, if a monk felt ready to end his life, he could elect to proceed to an underground chamber where he both meditated and slowly starved himself to death. His body was next smoked inside the chamber until it was moved to the temple.

6. B. After Osiris was dismembered by his enemy, she was able to piece him back together and become impregnated by him.

7. D. A place where, using the Book of the Dead, the deceased must account for their lives.

8. C. A dance performed by Native Americans to evoke the dead.

9. A. The ruler of the underworld.

10. C. It collects at the head of the person and remains there for three days awaiting judgment.

Returning to Nature

"Now comes the mystery."

Last words of Henry Ward Beecher

GETTING RID OF THOSE REMAINS

If a dead body is just left lying around, it won't be long before it starts to smell awful and look extremely gross. Nor will it take long for maggots and other hideous vermin to find it. We're talking seriously disgusting. And if the corpse happens to be your dearly beloved grandma this could be very upsetting, so finding a way to dispose of her is fairly important.

EUPHEMISMS

Last call
Lights out
Last bow
Last dance
Your number is up

What do you do with a dead body? The possibilities are endless. Excarnation allows humans to become part of the food chain by setting the body out for wild animals to eat. The Parsis in India (the only peoples known to still use excarnation) build special structures called "Towers of Silence" on which they place their dead, allowing vultures quicker, easier access. Although from an environmental standpoint this seems a natural and rather tidy way to get rid of a corpse, it is in direct opposition to preferred methods, which were designed specifically to avoid flesh-munching carnivores.

Going Underground

From simply tucking the cadaver into a cave and covering it with stones to interment in moisture-proof concrete vaults, burial has long been the most common way to dispose of the deceased.

Moms Mabley, outspoken as always:

"They say you shouldn't say anything about the dead unless it's good. He's dead. Good."

One good thing about today's burials are that the dead are truly dead. This hasn't always been the case. Before the advent of modern medical equipment, determining death was fairly unscientific business. Burial would take place if lemon juice squirted in the eye didn't cause a flinch or if a mirror held up to the nose and mouth didn't get fogged. Because these methods are somewhat unreliable, there are many tales of last-minute revival—people sitting up in the morgue, coughing or groaning during services, or knocking on the sealed coffin to get out.

Last words of Caligula, in what was only a momentary truth:

"I am still alive!"

Live burials were particularly common during plagues and epidemics because death was the expected outcome, and with so many people suffering from illness, everyone was short-handed. Fear of premature burial was so prevalent that requests ranging from amputation of a finger or toe to decapitation or disembowelment prior to interment were not unusual. In Victorian England, a special kind of casket and burial were used to allay fear. A string was tied around the deceased's finger. The string went through a hole in the casket and up a tube to the ground's surface, where it was attached to a bell. That way, if you happened to be buried alive you could ring the bell, alerting the graveyard guard to start digging.

Here are some disturbing tales:

- ❧ Minnie Keutsch was 17 years old when she "died" of typhoid. She was already sealed in her coffin when her sister, overcome with grief, begged to have another look at the dearly departed. Like some real-life Sleeping Beauty, Minnie awoke when her sister bent to kiss her farewell. Minnie lived until she was 99.

- ❧ In completely different incidents, Marjorie Elphinstone and Margaret Halcrow (both of Scotland during the 17th century) each had the good fortune of being buried with their jewelry; each was dug up by gruesome jewel thieves, and both Marjorie and Margaret revived during the robbery.

- In 1865, Max Hoffman of the United States, a five-year-old, was thought to have died of cholera. Two nights after the funeral, his mother had such vivid dreams of Max being alive in his coffin that she convinced her husband to dig up the boy. Sure enough, he was revived and lived until he was 90. Max kept the handles of his first coffin as a keepsake his whole life.

- And another man, who had typhoid, was pronounced dead and buried. Four days later he was exhumed for the bizarre fate of becoming a dissection subject in a nearby medical school. Just as the professor cut into the man's chest, he cried out and grabbed the professor's arm. The man later said that he was awake and aware during his wake and funeral but unable to move or speak.

But, back to burying people who are really dead.

Cairns (piles of stones placed on the body) were used both inside and outside of caves for centuries. As civilization developed, land-owning families usually set aside an area for burial plots. Others were buried in graveyards outside cities and villages. For the poor, there was nothing so fancy—just mass graves into which hundreds of bodies were dumped. Some of the mass graves in France hold up to 1,000 bodies each. Some 13,000 Union soldiers in a Civil War POW camp died of starvation and disease and were buried in trenches, 100 to a plot. The Black

---

YOU'RE NOT GOING TO WEAR THAT OLD THING, ARE YOU?

Archaeologists found a 3,500 year-old mummy wearing new clothes . . . Carbon dating proved the bandages it was wearing were put on some 1,200 years after the body had been embalmed.

Hole of Calcutta was used to bury anti-British rebels, sometimes while they were still alive. Potter's field in New York City is one of the largest mass graves in the world. It is estimated there are 150 bodies per marker. And at the end of World War II, thousands of unburied victims of the Holocaust were placed in mass graves by using bulldozers and tractors.

Last words of British Prime Minister Sir Henry Campbell Bannerman, in what was not the truth:

"This is not the end of me."

Early Christians, practicing an illegal religion, built underground catacombs which served as meeting halls, places of worship and a place to house their dead. Once Christianity became accepted, many congregations built catacombs under their churches, but they were used strictly as burial vaults. Bodies were interred in unsealed wooden boxes and crowded into damp basements. The heat, humidity, and vermin of the summer months meant that congregants often went to services and got a little religion and a lot of bacteria. By the sixth century, many Christians were going to their just reward a bit early as a result of attending mass. Even churches with outdoor graveyards had problems. It wasn't long before they ran out of room and were stacking coffins atop one another until bodies were just a few inches under the ground's surface, creating air and groundwater contamination.

But denial was never more clear than when Buffalo Bill Cody was told he was dying:

"Let's forget about it and play high five."

In America today, most people who choose burial get their own little piece of real estate in which to spend their eternal rest. But the peaceful serenity of modern cemeteries was a long time in coming.

Cities like New York, Boston, and Philadelphia had graveyards within

the city limits, but by the early 1800s, they were running out of space and the vile vapors rising from these stench-ridden areas were a serious problem. Then several epidemics struck, leaving thousands of fresh corpses to bury. For instance, in New York one outbreak of yellow fever killed 1,600 people in 1822. Officials began looking outside the city for a suitable place to inter the corpses and the garden cemetery was born. The first was Mount Auburn outside Boston, quickly followed by Green Wood in New York and then Laurel Hill in Philadelphia. These cemeteries were the first of their kind, lush with plants, trees, and grass. Replete with walkways and benches, they served as America's first parks and eventually led to the idea of municipal parklands in the United States.

Last words of Isadora Duncan, as she cheerfully bid goodbye to her friends and in what turned out to be too ironically true:

"Adieu, my friends. Off I go to glory!"

Glendale, California is home to America's largest cemetery. Forest Lawn opened in 1917 and has expanded through the years to encompass over 1,200 acres in four separate parks. A bizarre sort of theme park, Forest Lawn features a children's area called Lullaby Land, complete with a fairytale castle. Crypts are available in the New World section. Other themes include Westminster Abbey, Virginia Colonial, and Georgia Colonial. Today, Forest Lawn buries about 8,000 people a year.

But First . . . The Preparation

When faced with the prospect of burying a loved one, what should you do? Well, most people call a funeral director. The funeral director sort of acts as the host. He (or she, although most are male) coordinates all the details for the big day. Starting with transporting the body from wherever it expired and preparing it for viewing, the funeral director's job is full of gross, icky details. In many cases, a funeral director isn't really necessary, but most people want one because the who, what, where, how, and when of funerals and burials are not exactly common knowledge. Besides, most mourners do not want to deal with it. This has not always been true.

Last words of Murdering criminal Gerald Chapman prior to his execution:

"Death itself isn't dreadful, but hanging seems an awkward way of entering the adventure."

Family members used to prepare the body themselves, host the wake at home, and settle the details of a service and the burial. In recent times, people—especially Americans—have become very squeamish about death and the customs surrounding it.

But the main reason you need a funeral director is to embalm the body—not something you can readily do at home.

Embalming was first used by the ancient Egyptians. They took out all the major organs and preserved them in jars or urns, except for the brain—they thought it was just a useless mass, so they threw it away. After pouring perfumes, oils, and herbs into the body, they sewed it up, treated the body with preservatives, and wrapped it in cotton strips. Various methods of embalming were used until Pope Boniface VIII banned it for Christians in 1299, believing that the body would need all its parts for resurrection.

James W. Rodger, also a murderer about to be executed, was much more practical. Asked if he had a last request before facing a Utah firing squad, he replied:

"Why yes—a bullet-proof vest!"

In the early 1600s, shortly after the discovery of the circulatory sys-

Last words of
James French, executed in
electric chair in Oklahoma,
1966:

"How about this for a
headline for tomorrow's
paper? French fries."

tem, physiologist William Harvey got the nifty idea of replacing all the blood with chemical preservatives. But the notion was perceived as ghoulish, and it didn't really gain popularity for several centuries. Just before the Civil War, the concept of embalming reemerged with the discovery of formaldehyde. Once the war began, it proved a handy way to get dead soldiers from the battlefield to their homes for burial with a minimum of decay. Without embalming, soldiers had to be laid to rest on the battlefield because transporting the corpse was such a health hazard. Also, the poor guy would be quite repulsive by the time he got home.

Today, the usual purpose of embalming is to preserve the body so the family of the deceased can have an open casket at the wake and/or so that burial can be delayed for a few days. (It doesn't take very long for decay to set in—check out Chapter 4!) Embalming is, however, required if the death was the result of a communicable disease or if the body is transported over state lines. Although since there's a black market for everything else, perhaps nefarious truckers are willing to transport illegal corpses.

Murderer Neville Heath
asked for a drink before
his hanging:

"Ah . . . You might want to
make that a double."

Aside from draining all the blood and replacing it with a chemical cocktail, the body is also washed in disinfectant to kill maggots and mites and reduce odor. The anus may be plugged to prevent embarrassing gas leaks.

The mortician's job is then to make the corpse look as life-like as

---

KEEPING THE LITTLE WOMAN
AT HOME

In 1775, London dentist Martin Van Butchell had the body of his wife embalmed and put on display to increase the patronage of his dental practice.

Dr.s William Hunter and William Cruikshank not only embalmed the body, they used coloring in the preservative to enhance the corpse's life-like appearance with a rosy glow.

Londoners flocked to the exhibit and most likely increased Van Butchell's business. Detractors claimed a clause in the dentist's marriage contract provided Van Butchell with an income "as long as Mary was above ground," and demanded he give her a proper burial, but it didn't happen.

Eventually Van Butchell remarried and his new wife made Martin get rid of the curiosity. He sent the body to a museum, where it continued to draw spectators. In 1941, the body was destroyed when a bomb fell on the museum, essentially cremating her 166 years after her death.

---

possible. He will glue the fingers together so the hands look natural. Often, the eyelids are glued shut (who wants Uncle Jed's eyes flying open during the wake, scaring the mourners and possibly causing Aunt Minnie to have a heart attack?), but not before the mortician inserts rounded plastic disks to keep the eyelids from sinking. The most important and challenging chore is to get the mouth right. There are gadgets called mouth formers to help, but some morticians use barbed wire inserted into the gums. This is to achieve a natural, peaceful expression. (Real death expressions can be rather unpleasant.) Once the mouth formation is satisfactory the mortician will sew it shut, although some prefer to use Super glue.

A beautician will then do the hair and make-up. A nice coat of base and some rouge usually takes care of that ghastly pallor.

While the old saying goes "You can't take it with you," what you can do is be buried with it—whatever it is. For ancient Egyptian royalty, it was massive amounts of treasure, but today people are most likely to take the big sleep with their favorite things rather than anything of serious value. Some of the most common items placed alongside a corpse are sports-related—fishing poles, golf clubs, baseball gloves, etc. Pictures of family, favorite toys, religious memorabilia, or tools of the deceased's trade are also not unusual. Some people have made odder choices and have been buried with things such as televisions and automobiles.

Last words of Douglas Fairbanks, Sr.:

"I've never felt better!"

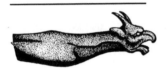

Here's a weird example of someone spending eternity with her favorite stuff. Margaret Thompson, a snuff addict who lived and died in Ireland in the late 18th century, instructed that her coffin be filled with Scotch snuff. The pallbearers all wore snuff-colored hats. The priest carried snuff and a procession of elderly ladies, all bearing enough snuff to get them through the service, followed. After the funeral, there was a party at Margaret's home at which 16 gallons of snuff were distributed to guests. The funeral was a weird exaggeration of the then-popular custom of placing a bowl of snuff in the casket with the body and allowing mourners at the wake to have a pinch. You could say Margaret was "snuffed out."

Once the dearly departed has been properly preserved, made up, respectfully gazed upon, and had his teddy bear tucked under his arm, it's time to seal the coffin and head to the funeral. But first a peek at what's happening to the old checkbook.

Embalming, flowers, church services, obituaries, limos, grave sites, burial vaults, and monuments can add up to enormous wads of cash. In fact, the amount you can spend is almost limitless. A casket alone can cost more than $30,000. Of course, you can select less expensive items and services.

Excluding a midnight trip to the dump (which is not only illegal, it's just plain nasty), a quick cremation and a memorial service in a park can usually be had for just a few hundred dollars.

Jane Ace:

"We're all cremated equal."

Burn, Baby, Burn

The idea of burning the dead as a method of disposal dates back to 1000 B.C. Funeral pyres were originally outdoor wood fires. Once there was a good base of hot embers, the body was tossed in to burn. It could take all day, but it was still considered a practical solution for soldiers who died in battle. In some countries, the funeral pyres of heroes and leaders were built on rafts and set adrift on the sea.

America's first crematory opened in 1876, but cremation was slow to catch on. It was considered gruesome and some religions, including Catholicism, believed it was sinful. In the past few decades, cremation has become much more common, especially on the West Coast. Although many religious leaders now accept cremation, the biggest factor for its increase in use is probably financial. Cremation is less expensive than interment.

Most of today's crematories are fueled by natural gas. The temperature of the oven will reach between 1,100° to 1,300° Fahrenheit. The body can be in a casket or a body bag when it is placed in the oven. A 180-pound man will burn completely in about an hour and a half. With older equipment, it may take up to three hours. The cremains (what's left after burning) weigh anywhere between three and nine

When his doctor said, "You are coughing with more difficulty," the dying John Philpot Curran, an Irish wit replied:

"That is surprising since I have been practicing all night."

Last words of
French scholar Bernard de
Fontenelle:

"I feel nothing except a
certain difficulty in continuing to exist."

pounds, with the average being five or six. They are quite gritty and can be gray, yellow, or white and will usually contain bone fragments. Most crematories will pulverize anything that isn't ash before returning the cremains to the family.

One of the problems with cremation is pollution, especially of bodies with a high fat content. They emit a greasy, black smoke so the ovens have to be outfitted with expensive after-burners and smoke-scrubbers. Pacemakers have to be removed prior to cremation because high temperatures cause them to explode.

If you have someone cremated, the ashes will be returned in a box unless you choose something else. A variety of urns are available through funeral directors and crematoriums, but you can have the ashes placed in any kind of container. Some people put the cremains of their loved ones in something appropriate to the deceased's lifestyle. Cameras, humidors, and cookie jars are just a few examples of things people have used. And there are jewelry makers who will put a little bit of ash into a tiny vial to wear around your neck.

What do you do with the ashes? Some people choose to bury them in a cemetery, some choose to keep the cremains at home. One popular idea is to scatter the ashes somewhere that has significance to the deceased. Despite the fact that the practice is illegal in some areas, cremains have been spread in many places— mountain tops, oceans, lakes, hiking trails, parks, and from airplanes. One woman, who loved to shop, requested her ashes be surreptitiously sprinkled throughout her favorite mall. Her daughter-in-law complied.

Probably the most famous distribution of cremains is that of Joe Hill. A labor activist who was convicted of murder and shot by a Utah firing squad, Joe Hill was then cremated. His ashes were mailed in small packets to union locals in every state except Utah and to every continent except Antarctica. On May 1, 1916, all the envelopes were opened and scattered.

There is a company in the United States that will reserve a place on a space shuttle, so you can have your cremains (or a portion of them) taken into outer space to become one with the universe. (Timothy Leary did this.)

Ahoy There, Matey!

Water burials date back to before written history. The long-held association between immortality and water led many cultures to dispose of their dead in oceans or rivers in the belief that this method would assure the return of a loved one.

Of course, there are those who have been laid to rest in the ocean without their permission, because it is a favored dumping ground for murderers. If a body is weighted properly and released in deep waters, it is likely to go unfound. But if it is dumped too close to shore or is too light, the tide will eventually wash the body ashore.

A legitimate water burial can be done two ways. Scattering the deceased's ashes into a body of water is by far the most common and is particularly popular in Asian countries. Burial at sea can also refer to the custom of slipping the casket or the wrapped and weighted body into the ocean. This used to be a popular burial for those who spent their lives on or near the sea. In Western culture today, burial at sea is usually only used for those who expire during an ocean voyage.

Last words of Scottish physicist James Cross, who had been a teetotaler all his life but requested a drink on his deathbed:

"I'll take a wee drop of that. I don't think there's much fear of me learning to drink now."

Hey, Save Me a Piece of That

While it is customary to dispose of the entire body when someone dies, there are, naturally, exceptions. Here are some examples of preserving a piece of history:

- Composer Joseph Hayden's head was stolen out of his grave by a guy who wanted to study the bumps on Hayden's skull. The thief was caught, but the head was passed around for the next 145 years. It finally came to rest with the rest of him.

- Albert Einstein's brain was removed as per his request. It was cut into segments and sent to various labs around the country for study.

- Three of Galileo's fingers are still hanging around. One of them is in Florence, Italy, where it resides in a museum, pointing at the sky.

- The brain of the father of modern brain surgery, Paul Broca, is preserved in Paris.

- In the midst of a religious war, St. Bonaventure's tomb was plundered. But someone saved his perfectly preserved head. It was considered an important religious artifact, but it was lost during the French Revolution.

Last words of German philosopher Georg Wilhelm Hegel:

"Only one man ever understood me and he didn't understand me."

THE FINAL GOODBYE

Funerals and memorial services, although centered around the dead, are really for the living. Traditions, prayers, and eulogies are helpful in allowing the bereaved to accept the demise of their loved one.

EUPHEMISMS

Gone to the races
Handing in your chips
Tossing in the marbles
Getting your ticket punched
Feeding the fishes

From a few words said over the grave site to hours of pomp and ceremony, the ways people choose to bid adieu to the dead are widely varied. Each culture has its own attitude about death.

On and off throughout history, black has been the color of choice for mourners. Originally, black was chosen because it was considered a good way to disguise the living from evil spirits or angry ghosts, which were thought to hang around death ceremonies. But red, green, violet, and blue have all enjoyed a turn at being the proper color to wear to a funeral. In China, it is customary to wear white. In Europe, black came back into vogue as the color of mourning around the 16th century (although in Spain, they had been wearing black since the 12th century) and has endured. Mourning clothes, regardless of color, used to be worn for extended periods of time—years in some cases, the rest of her life for some widows. But this tradition has, for the most part, been abandoned. In America, although black is commonly worn to funerals, anything conservative is acceptable.

X MARKS THE SPOT

From the Great Pyramids of Egypt to modern headstones, the living have long been making monuments to the dead. Prior to burial, caskets are often decorated with flags, blankets, or flowers. Once the deceased is interred, headstones allow loved ones to give artistic tribute to the dead, as well as to serve as a marker. The symbols carved on headstones have meanings. For example, the lily signifies purity, the willow means grief, a butterfly is symbolic of resurrection, and a crown denotes reward in heaven.

Some old tombstones are quite entertaining and show, in some cases, an almost flippant attitude toward the deceased, or even death. Tombstone epitaphs almost always rhymed, sometimes at the expense of truth. Here is a small sampling:

- In Skaneateles, New York:
  Underneath this pile of stones
  Is all that's left of Sally Jones.
  Her name was Briggs, it was not Jones
  But Jones was used to rhyme with stones

- In Pembrokeshire, England:
  Here I lie and no wonder I'm dead
  For the wheel of a wagon went over my head

- For a baby in Burlington, Vermont:
  Beneath this stone our baby lays
  He neither cries nor hollers
  He lived just one and twenty days
  And cost us forty dollars.

- In Cripplecreek, Colorado:
  He called Bill Smith a liar.

෮

෮ In Kent, England:
Fear God
Keep the commandments
and
Don't attempt to climb a tree
For that's what caused the death of me.

෮ For a baby in New Haven, Connecticut:
Since I was so very soon done for
I wonder what I was begun for

෮ In Dodge City, Kansas:
Played five aces
Now playing the harp

෮ In Ithaca, New York:
The pale consumption gave the fatal blow
The fate was certain although the event was slow

෮ For a family monument in Elgin, Minnesota
None of us ever voted for
Roosevelt or Truman

෮ From St. Mary's cemetery (1902 headstone) in Winona,
Minnesota
Killed by an unskilled doctor

෮ For a teacher from Elkhart, Indiana
School is out
Teacher has gone home

- From a tombstone in Girard, Pennsylvania
  In memory of Ellen Shannon
  Aged 26 years
  Who was fatally burned
  March 21st, 1870
  by the explosion of a lamp
  filled with "R. E. Danforth's
  Non Explosive
  Burning Fluid"

POP QUIZ

QUESTIONS (Answers start on page 61.)

1. The word "Willispanker" at a funeral refers to:
   A. A Southern tradition where mourners cirle the burial plot three times before the casket is lowered into the ground.
   B. A piece of Irish bagpipe funeral music.
   C. The fly-fisherman's tradition of being buried with a particular type of rod and reel.
   D. Nothing. It came out of one of the authors' demented imaginations.

2. What happens in the United States to the bodies of infamous serial killers or murderers after they are executed?
   A. They are cremated and the ashes are given to prison officials to dispose of properly.
   B. They are given to research labs where scientists study the physiology of the criminal brain.
   C. A current contract specifies that they be sent to London's wax museum where replica statues of the criminal are built.
   D. Any number of things, including being buried next to your Aunt Louisa.

3. Cats were revered in Ancient Egypt so when they died:
   A. They were buried in cat cemeteries.

B. They were stuffed (in what was the earliest form of taxidermy) and set outside to guard houses.

C. They were cooked and fed to other cats so their spirits were joined, making the living cats stronger.

D. They were used in contests where participants would swing the cat by its tale and fling it to see who could throw it the farthest.

4. The Chinese Heredity Jar is a traditional earthen container carried in funeral processions. One of its uses is:

A. To carry one drop of blood from as many relatives as possible, symbolizing family unity.

B. A children's competition in which each child tries to stuff the most food for the deceased into the jar.

C. To trade for funeral herbs at the burial site.

D. As a spitoon during the tobacco-chewing portion of the ceremony.

5. Charlie Chaplin's burial was unusual in that:

A. He was buried twice, the second time after his body was stolen and held for $600,000 ransom.

B. He is buried on a Hollywood studio lot..

C. While being interred, an earthquake shook the area damaging his casket. The proceedings were halted and it wasn't until the following day that he actually was buried.

D. In a salute to his most famous charater, The Tramp, he was buried in a pauper's grave.

6. For centuries the fear of being buried alive was so prevelant that in Europe there was a group called:

A. The Society for the Prevention of Premature Burial.

B. The Society for Beheading Before Burial.

C. The Check 'Em Once, Check 'Em Twice, Being Buried Alive Ain't Nice Association.

D. The Society to Ensure Death.

7. Cult leader Jim Jones's body was:

A. Sent to the University of Guyana where it was used for teaching dissection.

B. Buried in Forest Lawn in an unmarked grave.

C. Cremated.

D. Buried in Jonestown.

8. The highest rate of cremation is:

A. Among fire fighters, if you include volunteers.

B. In India.

C. Now among Catholics, who used to disapprove of it.

D. In Japan.

9. Where can you find the oldest active cemetery in the world?

A. Turkey.

B. Israel.

C. India.

D. In a strip of land between the Hatfields' and McCoys' property.

10. One of the largest segments of Einstein's brain can be found in:

A. Cincinnati, Ohio.

B. Edison, New Jersey.

C. Wichita, Kansas.

D. Hollywood, California.

11. In 1355, King Pedro I of Portugal did something very unusual when he assumed the crown. It was:

A. Exhume his dead mistress to have her properly honored as queen.

B. Kill all his children by burying them alive to prevent them from conspiring against him.

C. Force members of the court to eat portions of his father's body.

D. Hold a funeral for himself so he could enjoy the pageantry.

12. The word mausoleum comes from the memorial tomb of Mausolus, ruler of Caria, who died in 353 B.C. His widow had the tomb erected after she:

A. Began to feel guilty about killing him.

B. Received a telemarketing call from Tombstones R Us.

C. Had him cremated, mixed his ashes with water, and drank him.

D. Discovered she was expecting their child.

E. Realized she would be allowed to assume the role of ruler if her tribute to him was spectacular enough.

13. Excarnation, the practice of laying out a corpse for animals to feed on, was sometimes used:

A. To keep dangerous packs of dogs away from the living.

B. As a punishment to the dead and warning to the living.

C. To gain favor with vultures, who were thought to have magic powers

D. As a public spectacle, used to scare children into behaving.

14. The tradition of funeral wreaths originated from:

A. The belief that the dead could use them as wheels to get to the afterlife.

B. The Middle Ages when wreaths became popular for royal funerals.

C. A florist in the 1800s who, during an epidemic, didn't have time to fill all the requests for floral blankets.

D. The belief that the wreath would encircle the spirit of the dead and keep it at bay.

15. Long ago, people wore sack cloths and went barefoot to funerals. This was because:

A. They didn't want the dead to be jealous.

B. It was a sign of how poor their lives would be without the deceased.

C. They didn't want to capture the attention of the grim reaper.

D. It signified their subservience to the power of death.

16. Cryogenics is a fairly new science designed to freeze the body in the hopes that in the future the body can be unfrozen and reanimated. Ideally the freezing procedure should take place:

A. Approximately one month before natural death would occur.

B. Within 24 hours of death.

C. When the subject is still in good health.

D. Within 10 minutes of death.

ANSWERS

1. D. Nothing. It came out of one of the authors' demented imaginations.

   Oh, puh-leeez . . . a Willispanker?

2. D. Any number of things, including being buried next to your Aunt Louisa.

Most notorious criminals are buried in ordinary public or private cemeteries, but managers try to keep it quiet, mostly to avoid complaints from family members and vandalism.

3. A. They were buried in cat cemeteries.

4. B. A children's competition in which each child tries to stuff the most food for the deceased into the jar.

5. A. He was buried twice, the second time after his body was stolen and held for $600,000 ransom.

6. A. The Society for the Prevention of Premature Burial.

7. C. Cremated.

8. D. In Japan.

9. B. Israel.

The Mount of Olives in Israel is not only the oldest cemetery in the world, it is also considered a very holy resting place by Orthodox Jews. Many spiritual and highly revered leaders are buried there and people will pay as much as $20,000 to be laid to rest near a particular religious leader.

10. C. Wichita, Kansas.

11. A. Exhume his dead mistress to have her properly honored as queen.

Ines deCastro had been murdered and entombed two years before Pedro's coronation. Because she had been eviserated, her body was fairly well preserved. Pedro had Ines seated in the place of honor reserved for the queen. Loyal subjects bowed before the corpse and many kissed her shriveled fingers.

12. C. Had him cremated, mixed his ashes with water, and drank him.

Artemisia, who was both his wife and his sister, drank Mausolus and then erected a memorial tomb so amazing it became one of the sevens wonders of the world. It was built in Halicarnassus in Asia Minor.

13. B. As a punishment to the dead and warning to the living.

   At various times in different parts of the world, excarnation was considered a disposal appropriate for the disgraced. But other cultures (some Native Americans, for example) considered it the completion of a circle of nature.

14. D. The belief that the wreath would encircle the spirit of the dead and keep it at bay.

15. A. They didn't want the dead to be jealous.

   There was a belief that the spirits of the dead would only move on to the next life if nothing held them back. New shoes were particularly frowned upon at funerals because if the dead became jealous they would not leave the earth and would haunt the living.

16. D. Within 10 minutes of death.

   Companies such as Alcor in California will replace the body's blood with liquid preservative. The body is then moved to the cryogenics center where it is stored upside down in a container filled with liquid nitrogen.

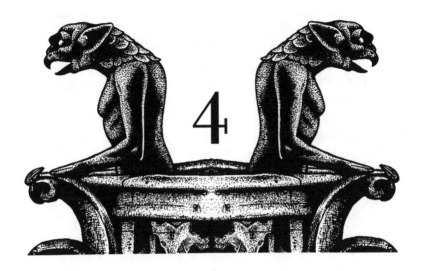

YOUR NUMBER'S UP . . .
NOW WHAT?

A friend came to view Callahan's body in the funeral parlor. He said to Mrs. Callahan, "Look at the beautiful smile on his face."

"Yes," she replied. "He died in his sleep. He doesn't know he's dead yet."

J ust like everything else these days, death is now a little harder to define. It used to be that if you didn't have a pulse, that was it. As black and white as that sounds, that is hardly the case today. No pun intended, but the definition of death has gotten a lot grayer over the years and can be found somewhere in the tangled fabric of medicine, ethics, and the law. With the rapid

A LITTLE DEATH HUMOR

A man who worked nights suspected his wife of being unfaithful. One night he left work early and, arriving home at two in the morning, found his best friend's car outside. He rushed into the house and into his wife's bedroom. She was awake, lying in bed naked, but reading a book. The husband searched everywhere but could not find a man. Finally, he went berserk, threw the TV out the window, then turned to the kitchen where he smashed all the plates and threw the refrigerator out the window. At the end of this performance, he shot himself. Arriving in heaven, he saw his friend, also waiting for admission. "What are you doing here?" asked his friend. The man described what happened, then asked—"but what are you doing here?" "I was in the refrigerator," explained his friend.

advances in medical technology, a person can be both alive and dead at the same time. The cause for this change in the way we define death is easy to track.

Back in the 1960s, two significant developments in the medical world occurred—organ transplants and life support. In 1967 in Cape Town, South Africa, Dr. Christian Bernard successfully carried out the first heart transplant. While the early survival rates for transplant recipients were quite low, today they are practically routine. Now, patients can successfully receive a new heart, liver, kidney, eyes, or even lungs. The problem, however, is that most of us turn chicken when it comes to checking organ donor on our licenses. People in need of an organ transplant can wait a long, long time.

The field of transplant medicine discovered that the chances for a successful organ transplant are better when the organ comes from a "live" body—the heart is still pumping and circulating blood through the body. The development of life support technology made it possible to keep someone thought to be dead alive. Today a person in a deep vegetative coma with irreversible damage to his or her body can potentially be kept alive indefinitely with life support. As a result, the perception of what dead is has changed forever.

So if your heart stops, are you dead? Technically no. Not if there is someone close by who can resuscitate you. Just like a stalled car, they can start you back up. In fact, there are situations when a surgeon will intentionally stop the heart during certain medical procedures.

With all of these technological advances, the definition of death had to be changed. Death is now perceived as a process. A person is considered dead if he or she is brain dead. Being brain dead is not that simple. There are three types which fall along a continuum. The first and least extreme is neocortical death, in which thoughts, pain, and pleasure no longer occur. Next is cerebral death, where only the lowest portions of the cerebellum and brainstem still work. Lastly, there is death by whole brain criteria. In the United States, a person can be considered dead if his or her brainstem no longer functions. In other words, nothing's happening upstairs in your brain and your heart and lungs can't function without life support.

We've all seen the episode on "ER." The handsome doctor strides in, checks the patient and says stoically, "He's gone." How do doctors know that with certainty? How do they know the person isn't asleep or just pretending to be in a coma? After all, it happens on soap operas every day.

Last words of Jimmy Glass, executed in electric chair on June 12, 1987:

"I'd rather be fishing."

Last words of Heinrich Heine:

"God will pardon me, that's his line of work."

EUPHEMISMS

Swimming with the fishes
Wearing cement shoes
Wearing a rope necktie
Kevorked
Doing yourself in

Doctors have specific formal guidelines for determining death. Here's a scenario: Let's say you slip into a deep coma and don't wake up. The doctor will routinely check you for evidence of six vital signs that indicate whether or not important bodily messages are being received by the brain. If you happen to test negative for all of them, the doctor will conclude that the vital areas of your brain no longer function and you have unquestionably "moved on." These six vital signs are:

1. The capacity to breathe independently. (Can you breathe without help?) The doctor will turn off your ventilator (if you have one) and then see if you can breathe by yourself.

2. Coughing or gagging. Coughing or gagging are involuntary or automatic reflexes that cannot be faked. The doctor wants to see if you cough or gag when your airway is suctioned out.

3. Pupils. (You want to get that light out of my face, buddy?) The doctor shines a light directly at your eye to see if the pupil constricts or gets smaller.

4. Blinking. (I hate when that happens.) The doctor actually touches the cornea of your eye. If you're alive, you blink. If you don't, well, you know the rest.

5. Grimacing. Although most people grimace when they get their doctor's bill, this is different. The doctor will at-

tempt to rotate your head or flush ice water in your ears to see if you have a normal grimace reflex.

6. Blood flow. In countries like Austria, Germany, and parts of Scandinavia, doctors are required to shoot dye into a patient to determine if there is still blood flow to the brain.

While most of us don't want a doctor touching our corneas or injecting us with dye, before the advent of these techniques, people were buried alive (see Chapter 3: Returning to Nature). Back in medieval times, people often requested slicing off a finger to prove whether or not they were really dead.

THAT FINAL CURTAIN

We can refuse to pay our taxes, skip church on Sundays or "forget" to return library books. But like it or not, dying is one thing none of us can avoid. Admit it, you've wondered how you were going to go. At the very least, we've all wondered how long we'll live. But consider it for a moment: What's it going to be like when you take your last breath? Will you know death is upon you or will you never know what hit you? Will it hurt? Maybe you'll be lucky and go the way everybody wants to go—in their sleep. Then again, you could be sitting next to some nut on the subway when he decides that it's "his" time to go. . . and take all the rest of the train with him!

According to the 1997 World Health Report, the leading causes of death throughout the world are: infectious and parasitic diseases, heart disease, cancer, and strokes. In the United States, most people die from heart disease.

What about AIDS? Four million people have already died from AIDS worldwide and by the year

Last words of
John Dryden:

"I'm trying to die correctly, but it is very difficult, you know."

2000, 30 to 40 million people are expected to test HIV-positive. And in the United States, AIDS is the leading cause of death in African-American and Latino men between the ages of 25 to 44.

Don't forget about cancer because its rate is increasing. Lung cancer is the leading cancer killer worldwide with cigarettes being the primary cause. In some circumstances, the job you choose can increase your risk of getting cancer. Your chances are three to five times higher if you work with vinyl chloride, asbestos, or rubber. In New York, carpenters and construction painters are at higher risk.

Some people die because, unfortunately, they are in the wrong place at the wrong time. The United States has the dubious distinction of having the highest murder rate in the developed world. If you feel your luck running out, avoid the District of Columbia, our nation's capital, because it is the most dangerous place to live in the United States. Also, scratch out the "Big Easy" New Orleans and Elvis's Memphis because they have the highest murder rates in the country. Feel like dusting off the

---

In the mood for a new puppy? Since 1990, over 50 people have died in the United States from dog attacks. Remarkably, just a few breeds are responsible for 98% of these deaths. While you may assume it's the rottweiler or doberman that is most likely to bite, there are seven other breeds more likely to take a chunk out of you:

1. Pit bull
2. German shepherd
3. Chow
4. Malamute
5. Husky
6. Wolf hybrid
7. Akita

passport and traveling abroad? The Philippines, Bahamas, and Zimbabwe have the highest murder rates in the world. If you want to play it safe, then head for Japan, the United Kingdom, Gabon, Ireland, and the Congo where murder is at the lowest. Some of us will die suddenly, perhaps in an accident, and have no idea what hit us—literally. Did you know that every 10 minutes, two people die in accidents in the United States? And don't run under a tree in a thunderstorm either. Ninety people a year are struck and killed by lightning in the United States. Thinking about leaving the city and becoming a lumberjack? According to the National Traumatic Occupational Fatalities, Alaska is one place where you could really hurt yourself—especially as a fisherman, logger, or forestry person. Maybe you want to break free from your rut and have some thrills. Your life insurance company won't be as enthusiastic and will either drop you or raise your rates if choose one of these pasttimes:

"On the plus side, death is one of the few things that can be done just as easily lying down."

—Woody Allen

- Car racing
- Ballooning
- Powerboat racing
- Scuba diving
- Horse racing
- Bobsledding
- Hang gliding
- Skydiving
- Parachuting
- Mountain climbing
- Bungee jumping

*Last words of
Marie Antoinette:*

"Farewell, my children,
forever. I go to your
father."

For the greater majority, we will pass away from some illness or old age. We are living longer than ever. Today the average person lives to be about 75 years old. In 1920, the average person lived to be just 53. If you plan on living a long life, it's probably best to live in North America or Europe where life expectancy is the highest. If you're not so sure, then head for lesser developed countries like Uganda with a life expectancy rate of 42 years or Sierra Leone where people check out at 39 years.

Some people have a different plan altogether when it comes to how they want to go. For these folks, they say to hell with it all and check themselves out. They must say that a lot in Sweden because they have the highest suicide rate in the world. Each year some 30,000 people in the United States toss in the towel and kill themselves. That's about one person every 20 minutes. Maybe it's time to start handing out the Prozac. Women try more often but more men are successful in actually completing their suicides. The popular methods of choice? Guys tend to reach for guns or some rope for hanging. Ladies, on the other hand, opt for a prescription drug overdose, inhaling gas, or cutting and stabbing. Still others choose jumping from a bridge or tall building, or drowning.

"We are here to laugh at
the odds and live our lives
so well that Death will
tremble to take us."

—Charles Bukowski

What does it feel like to actually die? For those who are about to die from illness, the jury is still not unanimous about what the soon-to-be deceased will experience. For one thing, what a dying person seems to be experiencing during the final moments can be very different than what is observed by the family or loved ones.

LIFE PICTURES

Some say that during a near-death experience, your life flashes before your eyes. In *Spiritual Awakenings* by Babara Harris Whitfield, an NDE researcher, an American soldier in Vietnam describes his NDE after he was shot: "I saw everything that had happened in my life. I saw myself as a baby, I saw the things my father did to me, and I saw a lot of things I really didn't want to remember . . ." (p. 58)

The actual moment when life is passing from a person can look like a physical struggle. In medicine, the physical struggle is called the "agonal moment." It happens because oxygen is leaving the body causing the cells to die. As oxygen leaves the blood, muscle spasms can occur. The dying person may start to gasp for air or even have a brief convulsion. Then it's all over and the person is gone. Naturally, this scene can be disturbing for loved ones who think that the dying person is suffering in his or her final moments. But as the song says, "It ain't necessarily so." It is suspected that the dying person feels a sense of peacefulness, total calm, and a sense of moving on.

But now to the good part. We all want to know what happens "after" we die. Where, if anyplace, do we go? Some party poopers maintain that dead is dead and there is no other destination. When you're dead you rot away and that's the whole story. They are, however, in the minority because three-quarters of the world happens to believe in reincarnation.

"It's not that I'm afraid to die—I just don't want to be there when it happens."

—Woody Allen

Still, people who die don't typically call back and tell how it all went, so we can't know for sure what a person experiences or truly

TOP 10 STATES IN DEATH RATES (1992)

West Virginia
Florida
Pennsylvania
Mississippi
South Dakota
Iowa
Alabama
Oklahoma

understands during the final seconds of death. No one knows what a dying person sees—if anything. Pearly gates? A guy in a red suit with horns and a tail? A room full of old relatives? The closest we have come is interviewing those who have been on the brink of death and then were suddenly brought back.

The near-death experience, or NDE, is debated by two opposing camps—the spiritual versus the scientific. The spiritual believe that during the near-death experience, a person actually gets a glimpse of the other side. That's how they explain why some people physically resist being saved or revived during a near-death episode. Many near-death survivors report being drawn to a white light so intense and inviting that it is irresistible. Others describe seeing themselves rise above their physical bodies only to be pulled suddenly back down. Some state they have seen loved ones or even famous people. The prevailing reports are that the experience is totally peaceful and euphoric.

Enter the scientists. Leave it to them to spoil the mood for every-

Last words of John Spenkelink, executed in electric chair on May 25, 1979:

"Capital punishment; them without the capital get the punishment."

body. They pooh-pooh all this talk of white lights, pearly gates, and cameo appearances of loved ones. Those starchy scientists explain that a dying person is feeling all warm and fuzzy because of changing neuro-chemical activity in the brain. The brain is telling the body to release endorphins, the opiates produced in the brain to reduce stress. The endorphins create a feeling of well-being.

"The fear of death is worse than death."

—Elizabeth Barrett Browning

According to a 1991 Gallop Poll, over 12 million Americans report having had NDEs. Here's what they reported:

1. The most common is feeling that you are leaving this world and entering another.

2. An incredible feeling of peacefulness so wonderful that you feel angry and resist if pulled away.

3. Like an old movie, your life passes before your eyes.

4. The out-of-body experience in which the person's astral body floats above their physical body, giving the person the sensation of flying.

5. Curiously, some NDE'ers can describe vivid details around them while they were unconscious.

6. Encountering other people such as deceased friends, relatives and historical or religious figures.

7. An ability to hear things that they could not have heard while clinically dead.

8. A brilliant white light.

9. A tunnel that leads them to another place.

10. Precognition: Though the least-reported, the claim of being able to predict the future after the experience.

THAT'S DISGUSTING. CAN I WATCH?

Once a body dies, it goes through some very gruesome changes. Forget about the old routine of getting cold, turning purple and stiffening up. That's kid stuff, everybody knows that. They never teach you in school about what happens in the minutes, hours, and days after a person is dead. Tick . . . tock . . . tick . . . tock . . .

Algor Mortis

As soon as a person is dead he or she starts to turn cold. Algor mortis is the term used to describe how the body temperature drops after death. A body's temperature will drop about one degree (F) per hour until it reaches the temperature of the air surrounding it. Just how fast a body's temperature will drop depends on how warm the living body was at death. If a person died in an unusual manner, such as in a frozen pond, the body temperature will be unusually low and it will be very difficult to know the exact time of death.

For dust thou art and unto dust thou shalt return.

—Genesis 3:19

Liver Mortis

Also known as the color of death, liver mortis refers to the settling of red blood cells to the lowest portion of the body, once the heart has stopped. The blood cells will settle to the lowest part of the body, such as the back, if the person is lying on his back. The remaining portions of the body grows pale as more and more of the blood cells sink. The settled red blood cells are called a lividity stain.

DEAD BODY FACTS

~ Insects and fish don't like embalming fluid.
~ A body decomposes much faster in water than on land—
four times as fast.
~ A body in outer space would start to mummify as it lost
moisture, becoming freeze-dried.

Two Hours

The skin starts to look reddish where the blood cells are settling. The area where the blood cells have settled becomes a deep reddish-purple color.

Eight Hours

The reddish-purple discoloration known by morticians as postmortem stain is permanent. (You go off to your eternal resting place with it.)

Rigor Mortis

The euphemism "stiff" for a dead body is actually the process of rigor mortis. After rigor mortis is over, the body completely relaxes and all the muscles sag.

Two Hours

Rigor mortis sets in about 2 hours after death—but it will occur sooner if a person is in the cold or was doing some kind of physical labor just before death. It starts at the same time throughout the body, however it is first observed in the jaws and neck.

TOP 5 STATES FOR SNOWMOBILING DEATHS

Michigan
Minnesota
Wisconsin
Illinois
Maine

---

12 Hours

A body's stiffness peaks after twelve hours and then turns limp as rigor fades.

12 to 48 Hours

The rigor mortis disappears entirely from the body.

Decomposition . . . Definitely Not for the Squeamish

24 Hours

If after 24 hours an undertaker hasn't started the embalming process, things really start to happen now. The body will now break down cell by cell.

2 to 3 Days

After 2 to 3 days, this poor soul starts to look very green around the gills. What's occurring is a lovely process known as putrefaction or rotting. It appears first in the abdomen, then chest and upper thighs. As if it's not bad enough that the person is turning green, you can bet that the body starts to smell pretty bad. That's because of the decaying red blood cells and—intestinal gas, which contains sulfur. The gas starts to spread out from the intestines, which causes the body to look bloated. Hold on, because things are about to go from bad to worse. Like air filling a balloon, the gas in the body increases until it forces the eyes and tongue to stick out from the face. This expanding foul-smelling sulfur gas forces the intestines out through the vagina and rectum. And for the finale—the green skin turns purple, then black.

Last words of
Anna Pavlova:

"Get my swan costume ready."

7 Days

After 7 days, this discoloration spreads over the entire body. Next come the bad-smelling blisters. Then the skin starts to peel off—in large pieces. And more bad gas.

Week Two

Everything is swollen and fluid begins to seep from the mouth and nose.

Week Three

By week three, hair, teeth, and nails start to loosen up. Then the internal organs start to rupture.

Two to Four Weeks

Finally, all that remains is a skeleton with skin.

The decomposition pattern of a dead body is central to forensic investigators who study murder cases. Skilled forensic experts can narrow down the time and cause of death in what seems like the most difficult of cases.

Last words of Leonardo da Vinci:

"I have offended God and mankind because my work did not reach the quality it should have."

AUTOPSY

An autopsy is the only way to know for certain how and when a person died. Like a road map of someone's life, autopsies give a vivid picture of how that person lived and died. Whether you're a fast-food junkie chomping on burgers and fries for years, or secretly been living in the fast-lane, your body can't keep a secret if there's an autopsy after your death. Autopsies play a key role in murder investigations and the trial that follows. A botched autopsy, like the one in O. J. Simpson's case, can send a trial into a tailspin.

Autopsies are not carried out just to solve a murder. They can also save lives by revealing dieting patterns or lifestyles of entire groups of people. Autopsies performed on soldiers killed in Vietnam revealed early traces of fat around their hearts, critical evidence that coronary disease is affected by diet early on.

Autopsies date back to the 14th century when physicians wanted to know the cause of a disease. During the plague in the 15th century, Pope Sixtus permitted medical students to perform autopsies to find out the cause of the deadly epidemic. Sometimes religion played a part in an autopsy. It is reported that the first autopsy of the New World was performed in 1533 to determine whether a pair of Siamese twins had one soul or two. The surgeon conducting the autopsy discovered that the twins were joined only at the liver, so it was concluded that two souls would need a posthumous baptism.

"It is impossible to experience one's death objectively and still carry a tune."

—Woody Allen

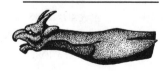

Today the rate of autopsies is declining in the U.S. With the tremen-

---

MOST DANGEROUS JOBS (1992)

Forestry Worker
Taxi Cab Drivers
Construction Worker
Truck Driver

---

dous strides in medical technology, autopsies are requested in only 12% of the routine hospital deaths. A physician must have a family's permission unless the death is considered suspicious.

Don't Try This At Home: The Autopsy Procedure

A typical autopsy takes about two hours but a criminal autopsy can take longer. A criminal autopsy can say a lot about how a person died, what was used to cause the death, whether or not the body was moved and if there's a cover up. A criminal autopsy gets down to the "nitty gritty" and can determine poisoning and DNA typing of the assailant.

The pathologist begins by stripping the deceased person bare and examining the outside of the body. Searching for anything unusual, the doctor will look in every nook and cranny. Bruises, swelling, bullet wounds, scratches or cuts, needle marks or any other marks are recorded. In the case of a female, a gynecological examination is performed and any evidence of semen will be gathered for DNA testing. The doctor takes scrappings from under the fingernails or samples from blood stains.

"Let us endeavor to live that when we come to die even the undertaker will be sorry."

—Mark Twain

Once the pathologist is finished with outer body, the internal autopsy begins. A "Y-cut" incision is made starting from the shoulders,

meeting under the breastbone, and continuing down to the pubic area. Next the breastbone is removed so that the doctor can see the internal organs. Sometimes the organs are removed and studied one by one. Thin cross-sections are cut and studied under a microscope. Fluid samples are taken to the lab for toxicology studies.

(Warning: Scaredy cats should skip over this paragraph.) Now that things are nice and messy, it's on to the brain. The pathologist starts with an incision to the back of the head, allowing the scalp to fold down over the face. Next a saw is used to open the skull. Once open, the brain is first observed in the skull then removed for examination.

Last words of George Washington, Dec. 14, 1799:

"I die hard but am not afraid to go."

The pathologist now has everything needed to determine the cause of death. The lab results of the organ tissues and fluids will help decide whether the death was natural or unnatural. Evidence found in the tissue cells may either support or contradict the suspected cause of death.

ANATOMY CLASS

Since the 18th century, medical students have studied the dead to learn about the living. The deceased or cadaver gives future physicians hands-on experience that textbooks can not. The cadaver is slowly dissected over one or two semesters. Students begin with the cadaver's back because it is more impersonal and it is a bigger area to learn about one's dissection tools. The head is the last portion of the body to be studied. When the school is finished with the cadavers, they are cremated and buried in a mass grave.

Today, most of the cadavers found in anatomy class are those of people who willed their bodies to science. Typically four students share one cadaver. The face of the cadaver is covered with a cloth soaked in preservative to both preserve it and to keep the cadaver faceless until the students become more comfortable with the dissection.

It wasn't always easy getting cadavers for medical schools. Up until the mid-18th century, medical students watched as their anatomy professor dissected one cadaver. Through

'The difficulty about all this dying is that you can't tell a fellow anything about it, so where does the fun come in?'

—Eugene Ionesco

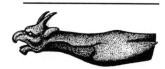

the centuries, some governments permitted hanged persons to be used as cadavers. But the demand for cadavers was greater than the available supply of dead criminals. In the 16th century, this problem led to grave robbing and many schools got cadavers in this way. Some medical students were forced to do a little grave robbing of their own because the school expected them to find their own cadavers for class.

In the past, the public thought it was scandalous to do dissections because it was believed that all the cadavers were the result of grave robberies. Some felt it was a violation of the deceased and disrespectful. The University of Maryland built underground tunnels to protect the anatomy classes. Hidden passageways allowed medical students to discreetly come and go from class.

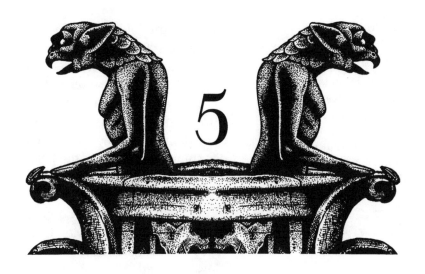

WHAT A WAY TO GO

"I did not get my Spaghetti-O's, I got spaghetti. I want the press to know this."

Last words of Thomas J. Grasso,
executed in 1995

DISEASES

Julius Caesar advised, keep your friends close but your enemies closer. While this might be good advice in politics, it is decidedly bad advice when speaking of man's biggest enemy—the tiny but deadly microbes that have been killing us off since we first roamed the earth.

Prior to modern medicine, doctors were pretty much stymied as to both the cause and the cure for illnesses that would take little more than a ten-day course of antibiotics to cure today. But

Last words of
Italian statesman Niccolo
Machiavelli:

"I desire to go to hell and
not to heaven. In the
former place I shall enjoy
the company of popes,
kings and princes, while
in the latter are only beg-
gars, monks and apostles."

back in the old days, doctors
thought up cures that smacked of
insanity and were often deadlier
than the disease they were trying
to combat. For instance, in
Shrevesport, Louisiana, they
burned tar and let the thick, black,
oily smoke fill the air in the belief
that it would keep yellow fever away,
not realizing the carcinogenic effect of such a pollutant. Covering
patients with leeches, giving them
repeated enemas, and draining
pints of blood, although thought
to cleanse the system, often hastened death because the methods caused weakness and dehydration.

Here are some of the bacteria and viruses that have been
most successful at reducing the world's population, along with
some interesting, albeit gross, information about them.

The Black Death

One of the worst was bubonic plague. This delightful disease
was characterized by swollen lymph nodes and quickly progressed to fever and delirium. Bubonic plague came from a
bacteria, which came from fleas, who got it from rats. Although
the rats seemed fairly unaffected by it, the bubonic plague (also
known as the black death) is responsible for killing hundreds of
millions of people. When you consider that the three largest
European outbreaks of bubonic plague occurred during the 6th,
14th and 17th centuries, when the general population was much
smaller than it is today, you can begin to understand how truly
horrific the black death was. In 762, an outbreak of bubonic
plague in China was so severe it killed one out of every two
people living in the Shandong province.

Although flea bites were the original source of the plague, many of the victims came down with pneumonia, which allowed them to spew out bacteria with coughs and sneezes, giving the germ a better stronghold.

The black death was usually found in cities where rats were plentiful and people lived in crowded conditions, all the better to hasten the spread of death. But occasionally, the disease wound its way into less populated areas.

One such occurrence was in England in 1665, when a man went to the remote village of Eyam with a bundle of cloth from London. Unfortunately, the cloth was infested with plague-carrying fleas and the villagers began to get sick. At the urging of the local clergyman, the village completely isolated itself in a heroic effort to keep the sickness from spreading. As a result nearly everyone in Eyam died. Ironically, most of the inhabitants would have survived if they had followed their instincts instead, which was to flee at the first sign of the black death. This is because had the village been abandoned, the fleas would have had nothing to sustain themselves and would have died off, eliminating the germ.

Industrialist Abram S. Hewitt removed the oxygen tube from his mouth and said:

"And now, I am officially dead."

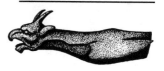

EUPHEMISMS

All washed up
Going to meet your maker
Gone to your final resting place
Laying down your knife and fork
Paying St. Peter a house call

The White Death

Tuberculosis was also a common cause of death. The oft-fatal illness is transmitted by inhaling the bacteria from an infected person's cough and results in respiratory failure. The heyday of tuberculosis was in the 1800s, when about 25 percent of Europeans died of it. Also called "consumption" and the "white death," tuberculosis actually became fashionable for awhile. The translucently pale skin and feverish reddening of the cheeks, along with the fainting and fragility of tuberculosis victims were romanticized by poets and writers as the epitome of feminine beauty. Talk about women dying to be beautiful. They say fashions are cyclical, hence an explanation for today's waif-like models.

But before the look of white death was "in," it was logically treated as something to be avoided. Probably in part because of the effect of tuberculosis on the skin, Hippocrates put forth the notion that tall, light-skinned blondes were natural carriers of the disease—stigmatizing Scandinavians for years.

The modern treatment for TB—antibiotics—not only virtually ended the threat of tuberculosis, it signalled the end of the numerous European and American sanatoriums originally built to house consumptives. Many of them, ironically, became fashionable hotels, health spas, and country getaways.

Don't Drink the Water

Typhoid is another bacteria our ancestors were lucky if they avoided. Related to salmonella, typhoid is a bacteria associated with contami-

nated water and/or food. It causes fever and fatally severe diarrhea. Nicknamed the "disease of filth," it was commonly found in crowded ghettos where sewage and drinking water intermingled. But typhoid and other forms of dysentery were actually responsible for much of the death toll in war. Soldiers were subject to unsanitary conditions and there are historical accounts of "bare-bottomed armies" and "breechless battles" because bacteria-ridden food and water made the men so sick. In fact, more soldiers died of illness than wounds in most of the battles fought before the 20th century. The discovery of antibiotics and the invention of more sophisticated weaponry tipped the balance in the 20th century so that more men died from traumatic injury than diarrhea. Not that it is of consolation to a guy who would rather not go into battle, but there it is.

Last words of Mongol leader Tamburlaine:

"Never has death been frightened away by screaming."

Typhoid and dysentery weren't only found on the battlefield, though. They were just about everywhere. Although diseased water is most often the source, in the case of Typhoid Mary, a human was the culprit. Mary Mallon, an itinerant cook, was an asymptomatic carrier of the disease. Her gallbladder was manufacturing typhoid bacteria, but she herself never had the disease. Not big on cleanliness, Mallon went from job to job spicing her dishes with death. Although the exact number of deaths attributable to her is unknown, she was the likely cause of at least 2,000. A doctor did eventually link her with a number of outbreaks, but she did not believe him and went into hiding, continuing to hire herself out as a cook under different names. She earned the title "Most dangerous woman in America," before she was finally caught and exiled to an island, where she spent the rest of her life.

From Innocuous to Devastation to Inoculations

As part of evolution, the human body will naturally develop an immunity to many of the diseases to which it is exposed. Of course, it takes quite a number of dead people to arrive at that point, but it is no doubt the reason why there were always those who did not succumb to whatever was going around the neighborhood. An interesting example of exposure and immunity is polio. A virus caused by exposure to infected human secretions, poliomyelitis has been around from at least the 4th century, but it wasn't until the 20th century that it really began killing people.

Last words of
Poet Dylan Thomas:

"I've had 18 straight whiskies. I think that's the record."

Prior to modern hygiene, and especially the invention of the flush toilet, the polio virus was quite common during the summer months. But usually only a few babies would come down with it, so it was known as "teething paralysis" or "summer complaint." By and large, the population was immune to the virus because exposure to the germ was so common. But a by-product of the more sanitary conditions of the 20th century was that people lost their natural ability to fight off the disease. Thus, at least 100,000 Americans were affected by polio. Although the majority of them survived the virus, most were left with permanent disabilities. The Salk (1955) and the Sabin (1961) vaccines ended polio's decimation by doing medically what the body had done naturally—creating immunity to the virus by introducing it into the system.

A Pox on You!

Smallpox is another virus over which medical science has triumphed. Tens of millions of people died of small pox, which at the least caused fever and terrible scarring, and often blindness. The first small pox vaccine was developed in 1796. Newer, improved vaccinations continued to eliminate the virus' potency. Today, there are theoretically only two samples of the live small pox virus. Both are in sealed test tubes: one in a laboratory in Moscow, the other at the Center for Disease Control in Atlanta. The last reported case in the United States was in 1949. The last reported in the world was in 1978 in England, when the virus accidently escaped from a research lab.

Last words of A French soldier:

"I did not mean to be killed today."

Esta Muy Mal

While most people have heard of the aforementioned diseases, the Spanish flu is not as notorious. And yet in 18 months, from 1918 to 1919, half the world's population was infected and some 25 to 37 million died of a virus which came to be known as the Spanish flu. Thought to have originated in the United States, the virus was an unusual combination of influenza and pneumonia that turned out to be the fastest moving, fastest killing plague in history. It was called the Spanish flu because Spain was particularly hard hit by it. As quickly as it came, the Spanish flu vanished.

No specimens of the Spanish flu exist. This is because viruses—especially flu viruses—can mutate quickly. Microbiologists believe it is this propensity to mutate that left

Dr. Joseph Green, an English surgeon looked at his doctor and said:

"Congestion."

Then, taking his own pulse:

"Stopped."

EUPHEMISMS

Gone to the pearly gates
Going home
Cloud nine
Buying the farm
Going belly up

them without a single sample of Spanish flu to study. It is also mutation that makes influenza such a continuing threat. For as the human body develops protection against a current flu virus, the virus can change, leaving the body defenseless against the newest genetic version.

While medicine has been somewhat successful in creating vaccines for influenzas, we are by no means guaranteed against them.

Love Ya to Death, Darlin'

And finally, you can't have a discussion about deadly diseases without eventually getting around to the sexually transmitted ones. AIDS is currently the biggest threat to those who engage in casual encounters, but sex has historically carried with it an element of danger. Prior to antibiotics, syphilis was not an uncommon way for people to die. Like AIDS, death from syphilis is a long, drawn-out affair that can start out with fairly mild symptoms and progress through the system until major organs are incapable of functioning. Starting with skin lesions, syphilis eventually affects the heart, nervous system, and the brain, often causing insanity before death.

During the 16th century, a drastic increase in syphilis cases gave Christian clergy an opportunity to preach chastity. They believed the disease signaled God's disapproval of promiscuity, which for many had become a way of life, and this helped establish the Puritan mindset in Europe during the Reformation.

The first treatment for syphilis was actually devised by barbers and bath attendants rather than doctors. It was called "the quicksilver cure" and entailed submerging the patient in a concoction containing mercury. While some people did get relief from the disease, the cure proved just as deadly, as the patient usually died of mercury poisoning—sort of like curing a headache with a bullet to the brain.

CAPITAL PUNISHMENT

Capital punishment has a long and twisted history, full of gruesome details. Although execution is legal in the United States today, it is usually only carried out after every appeal has been made. In addition, the manners in which criminals are put to death are those considered most humane.

This has certainly not always been the case. Stoning, one of the oldest ways to do away with the accused, dates back to the time of Moses. But it gained both popularity and status when St. Stephen, the first official Christian martyr, died in this manner. Like most capital punishments throughout history, it was done publicly to discourage unwanted behavior. In the case of stoning, the public actually participated. Usually held outside town, a crowd would gather around the accused in an area where rocks had been stockpiled. Starting with whomever was considered the victim (he who would cast the first stone . . .), the crowd would pelt the criminal with rocks. It was bad form to hit the accused on the head. Instead, the preferred method was to keep the victim conscious and

Last words of Beethoven after requesting a glass of wine that didn't arrive quickly enough:

"Pity, pity—too late."

Last words of
Ethan Allen on being told
the angels were waiting
for him:

"Well, let 'em wait."

try for as many broken bones and internal injuries as possible. The idea was that eventually the stoning victim would be crushed under hundreds and hundreds of rocks. If all went well, by the end of the ordeal, there was one dead criminal under a burial cairn made from the weapons of his death. Very tidy.

Snack Attack

The Romans considered capital punishment sheer entertainment. After the death sentence had been passed on several criminals (some of whom were considered criminals simply because they were Christian), it was time to take the family down to the Coliseum for an evening of fun. Thousands of spectators would watch as the unfortunate victims were sent onto the floor of the Coliseum to be eaten alive by hungry, carnivorous animals. While lions are most often cited in accounts of this blood lust activity, the Romans also used leopards, bears, and packs of dogs.

A Cross to Bear

Last words of
Elisa Bonaparte (sister to
Napoleon) in response to
being told nothing was
as certain as death:

"Except taxes."

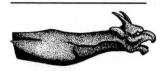

Crucifixion, another dreadful form of capital punishment, had already been around for ages by the time the Romans made it forever famous by using it to kill Christ. It is believed crucifixion was dreamed up by the Phoenicians, who then shared this gruesome activity with other cultures.

The Romans used it for the dregs of society—so that not only were the crucified publicly murdered, they had the additional degradation of dying by what was considered the lowest form of punishment. First, the accused were whipped, had shards of bone inserted under their skin and they were required to carry their own cross (or part of it if they weren't strong enough) to the execution site. Most criminals were tied to the cross, although really serious criminals warranted nailing. Contrary to the popular image of nails driven through the palms of the condemned, executioners found the delicate bones of the hands sometimes allowed the body to come loose, so they drove the nails into the wrists. Crucifixion was not a quick death. It could take three days for the victim to die. At the time of Christ, it was not unusual for authorities to wait until several people had been sentenced to die by the cross because it made a better public spectacle.

Last words of
Thomas Edison upon coming out of a coma:

"It's very beautiful over there."

The most ignoble of crucifixions was to be hung upside down. Ironically, considered worse than being hung right-side up, the inverted crucifixion was in fact more humane because death came more quickly.

More, More!

Capital punishment really became popular during the Middle Ages. The theory was that carrying out a death sentence in public would deter crime, but while crowds gathered to watch, pickpockets roamed among the audience working their tricks. So although the theory was obviously flawed, capital punishment became more and more common. Crimes such as criticizing the government, believing in the wrong religion, or even making too much noise at night could net the offender a truly painful death. Torture was in. Drowning pits, stretching racks, and hanging gallows were simply must-haves for every nobleman's castle.

Off With Their Heads!

Beheading enjoyed immense popularity and eventually became the most honorable method of capital punishment, often reserved for elite society. Many famous heads have rolled, and they were detached by an array of implements. Originally done with simple axes, the business of chopping off heads became so common inventors began mechanizing the chore and the Guillotine was invented.

An oft-told tale has Dr. Joseph Guillotin being prematurely born when his mother got horribly upset at a public execution and went into labor. Many historians contend that this is a myth, as is the idea that Guillotin invented the Guillotine—he didn't. It was created in a collaboration by a surgeon and a harpsichord maker, but Guillotin persuaded officials to use the machine because of its efficiency and people began to refer to it using the doctor's name. He fought the common referral until his death, but it never did any good.

Last words of
Football star George Gipp in a note to Knute Rockne:

"One day, when the going is tough and the big game is hanging in the balance, ask the team to win one for the Gipper . . ."

The thing about beheading is that if everything went well death was swift. But that was not always the object of capital punishment. Many methods were devised with express purpose of causing as much agony as possible.

Putting on the Squeeze

Pressing was one such punishment. It was often used to get a confession from a reticent victim. Used on both men and women, pressing entailed tying the arms and legs of the accused spread eagle to stakes and placing a board over their mid-section. Weights were placed one at a time onto the board. Victims were kept alive for days at a time and given food and water while their organs were slowly crushed. Pressing was particularly favored for those accused of treason because it was easy to get the victims to recant and apologize.

Franz Kafka didn't get his last wish, which was for friend Max Brod to destroy all his work:

"There will be no proof that ever I was a writer."

Ouch! That's Gotta Hurt

Then there were those who were drawn and quartered. In Russia, it meant each of the condemned person's four limbs were tied to horses. Each horse was then struck with a whip so that they ran off in four directions, literally tearing the victim apart. But to be drawn and quartered in Europe meant a different kind of show. Tied to a horse, the accused would be dragged from the jail to the execution site, but that was all the equine involvement for those folks. The victim would then be hung, but not to death. He had to be alive for the next stage—disembowelment. After slitting open the condemned man's belly, the executioner would yank out the intestines and toss them into a fire, hopefully while the victim was still conscious enough to watch. Decapitation, and mercifully, death followed. This lovely method was used mostly for crimes of treason. It didn't end in England until

"Most people would rather die than think; in fact, they do so."

—Bertrand Russell

Last words of Saint Lawrence as he was being burned to death:

"This side is roasted enough . . ."

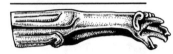

1870, when it was finally made illegal by an act of Parliament.

This'll Get You Steamed

Henry VIII executed some 72,000 subjects and gave credence to some even crueler methods, if you can imagine. In 1531, he made boiling people to death a legal form of punishment. The first person sentenced to die by boiling was, ironically, a cook. Convicted of preparing a poison sauce, Richard Roose was brought to the town square and lowered into a huge pot, where he simmered for a few hours before the temperature got high enough to kill him.

A Necktie Made of Rope

Hanging, always a popular way to kill a bad guy, has been around forever and has been used in almost every part of the world. It isn't particularly efficient, though. There are many accounts of multiple tries before the hapless criminals actually expired.

Up until fairly recently, "justice" in America was sometimes dealt by vigilante groups who engaged in lynching. Lynching supposedly got its name from a judge named Lynch who often ordered hangings. But the groups that lynched usually had nothing to do with the law. Without benefit of trial or evidence, they would capture and hang their victims, usually from a tree. Being suspected of a crime could net you a noose, courtesy of your neighbors, but so could being the wrong color or religion. Only four states can boast of its citizens never engaging in lynching. They are Massachusetts (where, although people weren't being lynched, they were being burnt at the stake), New Hampshire, Rhode Island, and Vermont.

Catching a Buzz

As for the government dealing out death as a punishment, early on, hanging was the preferred method. But as scientists experimented with electricity, it occurred to them that electric current might be a swifter, kinder means of execution than hanging, which was fraught with problems. Sometimes the rope broke or stretched, sometimes death was a long time in coming, sometimes it didn't even work. Inventor Harold Brown was working at Thomas Edison's laboratory in New Jersey and began electrocuting cats and dogs in the first electric chair prototype. In 1890, officials were ready to try it out on a human. William Kemmler was sent to the world's first electric chair in Auburn prison in New York. It didn't go smoothly. After the first 17 seconds of electricity coursed through Kemmler's body, the poor guy was still alive. The executioner tried and tried again until Kemmler finally went out, smoking, searing, smelling, thrashing, and convulsing the whole time. The entire episode took about eight minutes, which you would think would dissuade officials from their swifter, more humane theory, but nope. They had an idea and they were going to see it through. The next two electrocutions went pretty well. Then came William Taylor. He didn't die with the first current and the generator blew before they could zap him again. After giving him some morphine, they kept the

Last words of
A prominent French grammarian Dominique Bouhours, guarding the language to the end:

"I am about to—or I am going to—die. Either expression is correct."

Last words of
Movie star Bing Crosby, a devoted duffer to the end:

"That was a great game of golf, fellers."

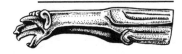

hapless Taylor alive for an hour and nine minutes until they could strap him back into the chair and give him enough electric current to actually cook him.

In 1903, Sing Sing prison officials electrocuted Fred Van Wormer. He was pronounced dead and taken to the autopsy room, where he revived. They called the executioner to come back to the prison and do his job again. Van Wormer passed away before the second electrocution took place, but they strapped him in and "killed" him again anyway.

Although the electric chair has continued to be a hotly contested method of execution (there are many stories of botched attempts), it is still used today. With more sophisticated technology, however, death in the electric chair usually comes in two to three seconds.

Cough, Cough, Gasp, Gasp

After the "success" of the electric chair, even better, faster types of executions were sought. Poisonous gas, which was used as a weapon in World War I seemed a dandy idea to some. Ironically, the chair was invented as a better alternative to hanging or beheading and the gas chamber was supposed to be an improvement over the chair. But the chamber proved to take longer on average (eight to nine minutes) and was apparently even more painful than the chair, while a properly done beheading causes instantaneous death. The gas chamber, first used in 1924, is

I am thy father's spirit,
Doomed for a certain term
to walk the night;
and for the day confin'd
to fast in fires,
Till the foul crimes done
in my days of nature
Are burnt and purg'd
away.

—Ghost of Hamlet's father,
Shakespeare's *Hamlet*

EUPHEMISMS

Gone to your reward
Hanging up your hat
Stepping off the edge of the carpet
The journey's end
The debt we all must pay

---

still in use today, although it has improved. It, too, has drawn a lot of criticism because it is believed that death by gas is incredibly painful.

A Shot in the Arm

Lethal injection was used for the first time in 1982. Because it uses three drugs, starting with a barbiturate that causes the victim to lose consciousness, death by injection is both quick and painless. Aside from the debate about the morality of capital punishment, lethal injection has raised another question of ethics. Unlike other death sentences, which are carried out by executioners, lethal injections are administered by doctors. Since doctors are suppose to adhere to the Hippocratic oath, and participating in capital punishment is in direct opposition to the oath, the issue has made for many arguments.

And Now That We're Completely Civilized

Currently 37 states in America allow capital punishment, although legislation is pending in a few more. There are five accepted methods, but state by state the methods vary. By far, lethal injection is the most commonly used. Thirteen states use the electric chair. New Hampshire, Montana, and Washington allow hanging, but from 1977 to 1995 only two people were hung, both in Washington. Those three states also offer lethal injection, as do the states that have a gas chamber. Although death by firing squad is acceptable in the United States, only the state of Utah uses the method.

KILLING THE MASSES

Genocide is an attempt to eliminate an entire group. The Holocaust in Germany between 1933 and 1945 is the largest single case of genocide in history. The Nazis tried to demolish the Jewish population, managing to kill about 6 million. They used gas chambers, guns, and bombs to murder people, but many others died of starvation and sickness while in work camps. Many other non-Aryans were also killed during the Holocaust. Some people, especially twins, were reserved for bizarre, tortuous "medical experiments," from which many of them died. While the Holocaust remains the most well-known attempt to eradicate an entire people, it certainly isn't the only one.

From 1876 to 1896, the Turkish Army tried to eliminate the Bulgarian peasants. They killed over 12,000. Turkish armies also tried to wipe out Armenians during World War II. The death toll was somewhere between 600,000 and 1 million. In Cambodia between 1975 and 1977, Pol Pot ordered the death of 2 to 4 million people for political reasons. And between 1991

WHO BUILT THIS DAMN THING, ANYWAY?

A combination of nature and poor construction killed 2,300 people in Johnston, PA. After a heavy rain, 20 million tons of water broke through a faulty dam and flooded the town in 1889.

and 1995, Bosnian Serbs killed some 250,000 Bosnians and Muslims in the name of "ethnic cleansing."

War, regardless of whether it has been connected to genocide, has always been responsible for considerably lowering populations. The biggest death toll was World War II, when 15 to 20 million military lives were lost, but more shocking is the over 25 million civilians that were killed. World War I had the next highest number of fatalities with 14 to 15 million. The Korean Conflict was responsible for the demise of between 2 and 3 million, and approximately 3 million people died during the Vietnam War.

> Oh Heavens! What do I feel? An invisible Flame scorches me, I can bear it no longer, my whole Body is a burning Fire-brand. Oh!
>
> —Moliere, *Don Juan*

Don't Invite These Guys Over for a Game of Trivial Pursuit

Serial killers such as Ted Bundy and Jeffery Dahmer have achieved notoriety for claiming multiple victims, but other guys have racked up far higher numbers by making a career out of murder. Dr. Marcel Petiot liked to inject poison into people. He was convicted of 27 deaths but thought to have killed 67. In Germany, Ludwig Tussov murdered and dismembered an estimated 30 children, and Bruno Ludke killed approximately 85 women. Ludke himself died in a medical experiment. Pedro Lopez strangled young women for fun. He claimed responsibility for about 300, all over South America. In the United States, Henry Lee Lucas confessed to 360 murders but police have only attributed 147 to him. And Fras Hooijaijers, a Dutchman, injected some 259 nursing home patients with deadly doses of insulin.

They groaned, they stirred,
they all uprose,
Nor spake, nor moved
their eyes;
It had all been strange,
even in a dream,
To have seen those dead
men rise.

—Samuel Taylor Coleridge,
from "Rime of the Ancient
Mariner"

Sometimes masochists have been in powerful positions and have used their authority to satisfy their lust for pain and/or blood. The Roman Emperor Caligula so enjoyed watching torture and death that he often dined or had sex while his officers mutilated and murdered people in front of him.

Giles deRais, Marshal of France during the 15th century, killed over 800 young boys in a gruesome variety of ways. But Vlad the Impaler probably wins the award for the most astonishing array of torture. He killed thousands of "enemies," and his favorite method—from which he received his name—was to impale them on stakes. Vlad (or would that be Mr. Impaler?) became the model for the original Dracula myth.

In 1600, Elizabeth Bathoy, a Hungarian Countess, ordered young virginal women killed and drained of blood so that she could bathe in the blood, thinking this would help her retain her youth. She slaughtered some 650 girls. "The Blood Countess," as she came to be called, is believed to be a direct descendant of Vlad the Impaler.

THE TINIEST VICTIMS

Widely accepted in earlier times, infanticide describes the act of a mother killing her own baby. In some cultures, infanticide was considered a prayer. Firstborns were often sacrificed in the hopes of gaining approval from various gods. The babies died by fire or poison drops the mothers would put on their nipples before nursing.

Infanticide has also been, at various times throughout the world, an acceptable form of population control. The tiny victims were almost always females. But by the 20th century, only natives of India and China still engaged in the practice with any regularity.

In many places, multiple births were considered either animalistic or an ill omen and necessitated killing off the extras. In Venezula, keeping a multiple birth a secret and killing a twin or two triplets kept the family honor intact.

Last words of
Frederic Chopin, dying of tuberculosis:

'The earth is suffocating . . . Swear to make them cut me open, so that I won't be buried alive."

Because of the associated disgrace, unwed mothers often killed newborns without hestitation. The practice was illegal by the Middle Ages, but that didn't mean out-of-wedlock babies were any more accepted, so the infanticide continued. Feudal lords had the right to rape peasant girls who worked on the estate but were not obligated to accept any responsibility for pregnancies that resulted. In addition, soldiers had the same rights. The effect was countless infants birthed and killed by poor young women stuck in a no-win situation.

MUST HAVE BEEN IN THE WRONG PLACE AT THE RIGHT TIME

Sometimes it seems as if Mother Nature is just plain pissed off. At least, that's the way it seems to man, who has done battle with the power of forces completely out of his control. Too much water, not enough water, tiny bacteria, angry mountains, furious seas, and serious winds have all taken their toll on the world's population. Despite technological advances that allow us to foresee and sometimes prepare for earthquakes, hurricanes,

"Health nuts are going to feel stupid one day—lying in hospitals dying of nothing."

—Redd Foxx

tornadoes, and volcanic eruptions, Mother Nature remains untamed. We are still occasionally taken by surprise and the cost can be thousands of lives and hundreds of millions of dollars in property damage.

When Hurrican Andrew hit the United States in August of 1992, Florida residents knew the storm was headed their way and that knowledge precipitated the largest mass evacuation in history. But the swath of destruction the hurricaine left was still shocking—billions of dollars worth of property damage. Because of the forewarning, only 44 deaths are directly attributed to Andrew.

The technology that allows us to see a big one coming is relatively new. History is littered with devastation from hurricaines, tornados, and cyclones that racked up astonishing death tolls. One all-star storm took place in 1737, when the water level at the Bay of Bengal in India rose 40 feet and caused 300,000 deaths.

Heavy rainfall or snows are often at the root of avalanches, another one of Mother Nature's tricks. As snow (or rocks, mud, or ice) builds up on a steep mountain slope, the danger of an avalanche increases. Eventually, like the proverbial straw on a camel's back, one more rain or snowfall starts massive downhill movement. Avalanches can also be caused by tremors or vibrations when tons of loose material is precariously perched on a slant. Avalanches have buried many an unsuspecting victim. For example, over 20,000 inhabitants of Yungay, Peru died when a giant mud slide covered the city with 76 million cubic meters of mud, ice, and snow.

"There's one way to be born, but there are thousands of ways to die."

—Anonymous

But avalanches are only one way mountains lord their awesome power over man. Some peaks are alive with active volcanoes, ready to spew their fiery death on life below.

But why do spirits walk the earth, and why do they come to me?

—Scrooge, from Dickens's *A Christmas Carol*

Two of the most famous volcanic eruptions are Vesuvius and Krakatoa. Mt. Vesuvius erupted in 70 A.D. and completely buried the city of Pompeii under tons of mud and volcanic ash. Fifteen thousand

of the city's 20,000 inhabitants died instantly. When archaeologists uncovered the city, they found skeletons and petrified bodies in the midst of everyday activities, such as sitting at the dinner table. Krakatoa, which literally exploded in 1883, had an even higher death rate—36,000. Krakatoa is located in Indonesia but the explosion was so loud it was heard in both Texas and Australia. A cloud of ash covered the area and took so long to clear that there wasn't true sunshine for a year. The ash cover was also blamed for snow in the United States during July of that year.

You would think that the geologic equipment of the 20th century would ensure enough advance warning to prevent such high numbers of casualties. While this was true when Mt. St. Helens spewed out enormous amounts of rock, smoke, and ash in the early 1980s, consider that in 1985, 30,000 people died in a series of volcanic eruptions in South America.

Mother Earth doesn't just wreak havoc from on high. Small shifts in the earth's tectonic plates can cause devastating earthquakes. One of the worst occurred in Tokyo in 1923, when 300,000 people perished.

Scientists have identified seven major tectonic plates on the earth's surface. While living on the edge of one of these plates (the San Andreas Fault in California, for example) is probably risky, living far away from them is no guarantee you'll never experience an earthquake. "Maverick quakes" often occur in areas that seem geologically stable.

Earthquakes are far more common than most people realize, because many of them occur in remote areas or are very subtle. But when two plates grind against each other in highly populated, densely developed places, the cost to humans can be huge.

In the United States, the San Francisco quake of 1906 is one of the most notorious. It caused a previously unheard-of amount of property damage. It doesn't, however, rank high on the death scale—500 people all told. Interestingly, 200 babies were born during the disaster.

Oops!

Calamities are not always the work of nature. Since the existence of mass transportation, accidents have meant multiple deaths. Many passenger ships have sunk, carrying their human cargo to a watery grave. The most famous, of course, is the Titanic, which took over 1,500 lives with it when it went down. But with the invention of the steam engine, railroads began racking up their own victims. One of the biggest train wrecks in history was in 1917 when a French train crash wiped out 550 folks.

All houses wherein men
have lived and died
Are haunted houses.

—Henry Wadsworth Longfellow, from "Haunted Houses"

In today's world, most people associate mass transportation catastrophes with airplanes. For when man goes up, he must come down. And that doesn't always happen with a neat, orderly landing. From crafts like the Hindenburg to unfortunate space missions, occasionally technology fails and disaster follows. Statistically, it is safer to ride in a plane than in an automobile, but the fear of flying is so common that in any city you can find a number of classes, therapists, and hypnotists dedicated to combatting the flying phobia.

The fear of flying probably stems from a number of things, including tight spaces, lack of control, and the seemingly unnatural act of a huge heavy plane flying through space. Last, but certainly not least, is the incredible spectacle of plane crashes.

> The greatest punishment God can inflict on the wicked, is when the church, to chastise them, delivers them over to Satan, who, with God's permission, kills them, or makes them undergo great calamities.
>
> —Martin Luther, *Table Talk*

As of the writing of this book, the worst air disaster in history was the result of pilot error. In 1977, a KLM plane collided in midair with a PanAm flight, killing everyone aboard both planes. A total of 580 died in the disaster.

Airplane crashes have had their moments of irony. A TWA Super Constellation and a United DC-8 jet crashed into one another over Staten Island in December of 1960. The United plane fell from the sky and embedded itself in The Pillar of Fire Church. As if that wasn't weird enough, four years earlier, planes belonging to the same two airlines collided over the Grand Canyon and the same number of people died in that accident.

TWA flight 800, which exploded over New York just minutes after it took off, was ironically piloted by Ralph Kevorkian. The name Kevorkian has become closely associated with death because of Dr. Jack Kevorkian's efforts to legalize physician-assisted suicide. The two were not related.

UNUSUAL, UNLIKELY, AND UNPLEASANT DEATHS

Since man has been doing it since life began, there are bound to be some strange ways that people have died. By their own hand, at someone else's, by forces of nature, and by freak accidents, some tales of demise are hardly believable. Here is a small sampling of some odder circumstances.

- In Downingtown, Pennsylvania, a man working at a cookie factory drowned when he fell into a vat of chocolate. His name was Robert Hershey.

- Talk about a deadly slice! Michael Scaglione was playing a round of golf in New Orleans when he got so angry with himself over a bad shot that he threw his golf club, which broke when it hit a golf cart. The club head snapped off and bounced back, hitting Scaglione in the throat. It severed his jugular vein and killed him. He was on the 13th hole when it happened.

- David Grundman fired two shotgun blasts into a giant cactus in the Arizona desert. While he successfully killed the cactus, the cactus got revenge when it fell on top of Grundman, crushing him to death.

- Here's a tale of family fate. Erskine Lawrence Ebbin was killed when he was run over by a taxi in Bermuda. Exactly one year later, the same cab driver, carrying the same passenger, struck and killed Erskine's brother, Neville.

- In Barcelona, Spain, a passenger on a bus decided to escape the crowd and climbed on top of the vehicle where he discovered an empty casket. He then decided to avoid the rain by climbing in and closing the lid. Two other passengers made their way to the bus's roof and after awhile the man in the casket opened the lid to ask if the rain had stopped. The other two roof riders were so startled they fell off the moving bus. One of them was killed.

- A woman in Warsaw, Poland, got so upset when her husband told her he was leaving her that she went out onto their tenth story balcony and jumped. She survived, however, because she landed on a man who was coming out of the building. He was killed. The man? Her husband.

🙵 Sometimes a food doesn't have to be a part of your diet to kill you. John Ramsey worked at a factory in Baltimore until he fell into a cole slaw mixer and got blended to death. Nazar Zia was at work when she fell into a vat of gravy and drowned. And Charles W. Doak, the president of the Wilson Candy Company, was beaten to death with a nine-pound candy cane.

🙵 Dr. Alice Chase, author of *Nutrition for Health* died of malnutrition. Another nutrition expert, J. I. Rondale was being interviewed on *The Dick Cavett Show* when, minutes after announcing his health was so good he expected to live a very long life, he dropped dead.

🙵 In Montreal, Antoine Blisonnette was literally bored to death. She was at work when she yawned and her mouth got stuck open. She had to have corrective surgery and later died of complications.

🙵 While it is commonly thought that laughter is good for what ails you, the fact is there are a number of documented cases of people laughing themselves to death. The actual cause is a heart attack or choking, but it started with laughing. One oft-cited case involves Alex Mitchell, an English bricklayer, who went to paroxysms of laughter while watching a sitcom called *The Goodies*. After a half-hour of uncontrollable laughing, he died of a heart attack.

🙵 Some things are destined to happen even when it seems at first that fate has been avoided. Such is the case of a Texan named Henry Ziegland, who first avoided serious injury when the brother of his jilted lover came calling for revenge. Although the brother shot at Ziegland, the bullet missed and lodged in the trunk of a nearby tree. But 20 years later, the attempt met with success. Ziegland wanted to remove the tree but rather than cut it down, he decided to dynamite it. The explosion sent the bullet flying out of the trunk and it hit Ziegland in the head, killing him instantly.

<ul>
<li>And then there are the cases of death being foretold. King Ferdinand V of Spain was informed by a fortune teller that he would die in Madrigal so he took care to never visit there. But he got sick in a small village and died of fright when he was told the village was known as "Little Madrigal."</li>

<li>The same thing is true for King Henry IV of England who had been told he would die in Jerusalem. One day the king went into an epileptic fit and was carried into a room in Westminister Abbey. When he found out he was in the Jerusalem Room, the shock killed him.</li>

<li>Oh, the burden of money! Hrand Arakelin probably thought if he died on the job, it would be at the hands of a thief. He worked on an armored truck guarding money. But his demise came one day when he was riding in the back and the truck swerved. Over $50,000 in quarters shifted and crushed him to death.</li>

<li>Eleven homeless men in New York City turned bright blue, and one of them died. At first, physicians were baffled as to why the victims were such an odd hue. Eventually, they figured out that each of the men had eaten at the same restaurant where sodium nitrate had erroneously been used in place of salt. Although many people had gotten a small dose, the 11 men, all of whom were alcoholics and therefore craved salt, sat at the same table throughout the morning and added excessive salt to their oatmeal. The extra "seasoning"</li>
</ul>

brought the men's sodium nitrate to a toxic level and poisoned them. They turned blue from the lack of oxygen in their blood.

~ Another homeless man, Pat Burke of St. Louis, Missouri, died from cleanliness. He was at the city hospital when hospital personnel decided to give him a bath—his first in 20 years. He died shortly after because the attendants had scrubbed him with brooms, which apparently caused an infection that went untreated.

~ What a CATastrophe. Henri Villette of France tied an unwanted cat into a bag and tried to drown it by tossing the bag into a river. But he slipped and fell in the water, drowning himself. The cat escaped and swam safely ashore.

~ Talk about loving someone with all your heart. In 1985, 14-year-old Donna Ashlock of San Francisco desperately needed a heart transplant. Her boyfriend, Felipe Garza, 15, told his family that Donna would live because he would die and donate his heart to her. Although he was perfectly healthy, he dropped dead from a blood clot in his brain within two weeks. Felipe's parents, who didn't know Donna, mentioned their son's wish to the doctors. It turned out the the couple was a good match and Felipe's heart was transplanted into Donna. The operation was a complete success.

~ In what is truly a piece of "twisted" trivia, here is a hideously gruesome fact. Occasionally people fall or are shoved into or under oncoming subway trains. It is a swift and far more merciful death for those who end up under the train wheels. Some people who have fallen into moving trains have been known to get caught between the cement platform and the moving cars. This has, on occasion, resulted in the lower part of the body being twisted around like a rubber band. Because the train acts as a tourniquet in this scenario, the victim may be conscious, clear thinking, and relatively pain-free as the upper part of the body continues to function. Within seconds of freeing the victim, however, he or she will die. Unfortunately, it can take hours and a huge effort to free such a victim—while everyone involved knows the outcome.

- Twelve hundred Turkish prisoners died in 1799 when, after Napoleon decided to set them free, he complained about a coughing fit. But his words—"Ma sacree toux," (my confounded cough) were misunderstood. The officers heard "Massacrez tous" (kill them all) and opened fire, killing all the prisoners.

- What, exactly, did he expect? Illusionist Chung Ling Soo had two of his assistants shoot him. They did. He died. Of course, that wasn't supposed to be the outcome. Although newspapers speculated on rumors of suicide and murder, the truth is, it was just a trick gone bad.

    Although the riflemen loaded their guns in front of the audience, there was a block between the firing pin and the bullet so the gun wasn't supposed to actually fire. But a tiny amount of gunpowder had slipped into a tube beneath the gun's barrel, detonated from the spark of the firing pin and shot a bullet into the illusionist's head.

- And what did these guys expect? In 1971, some scientists decided to study an area of Japan where frequent landslides were a problem. To mimic natural landslide conditions, they began soaking a steep hillside with water hoses. While they were successful in their endeavor, they didn't have much time to do their studies because the ensuing landslide killed 15 and injured 10.

✤ Here's a case of someone dying without the benefit of death. Jonathan Swift, author of *Gulliver's Travels* wrote a book called *Predictions for the Year 1708* under the pseudonym Issac Bickerstaff. In it, he predicted the death of rival John Partridge to the hour.

Partridge didn't even get sick on schedule but "Bickerstaff" and his cronies claimed Partridge had passed away exactly as predicted. They even published a pamphlet saying "Bickerstaff's" prediction was true. It went on to claim that on his deathbed, Partridge admitted he himself had been a charlatan. (Both "Bickerstaff" and Partridge were well-known psychics.)

Partridge then took out a newspaper ad protesting that he was still alive. And although he lived for seven more years, Partridge spent a great deal of that time trying to prove his own existence. He died without ever learning the true identity of "Bickerstaff."

✤ Spontaneous Human Combustion (SHC) is a strange phenomenon that may or may not be real. Striking without warning, SHC causes a human being to suddenly burst into flames and incinerate completely within a few minutes without affecting the victim's environment. There are about 200 documented cases of SHC, but some scientists claim none of them are real.

Those who have studied human combustion have come up with a variety of explanations. The original theory was that SHC happened to obese people who were either alcoholic or took baths in alcohol. They thought the combination of fat and alcohol made a person extremely flammable. Another idea was that those who became victims of SHC had a high phosphorous content in their systems. An enormous build-up of static electricity in the body has also been blamed. Then there are those who believe it is caused by alien invasions or black magic.

In 1725, a court admitted internal fire as a credible defense in a case when a man was accused of burning his wife to death, and he claimed it was spontaneous human combustion. Stories of SHC include some bizarre details like victims being in a locked room, one part of the body remaining completely unburnt and bodies that have been incinerated at such a high temperature that they have been carbonized.

~ In India, a bride whose dowry does not measure up can be murdered. Either the groom or his family can decide (after the marriage is complete and the dowry has been given) that the dowry is not acceptable and kill the woman by setting her on fire. When a bride is the victim of dowry death, the groom and his family can keep the dowry and look for a new bride.

While you might think dowry death is something out of the Middle Ages, there were 20,537 recorded dowry deaths in India between 1990 and 1994. Although the tradition is not really legal, it is often not prosecuted either.

~ Bite me, dough boy. Fairy tales are ripe with the threat of cannibalism. Hansel and Gretel, Jack and the Beanstalk and the original stories of Sleeping Beauty and Little Red Riding Hood all carry the theme.

Today it is generally associated with very uncivilized remote areas or satanic cults. But cannibalism has a place in humanity's history. The Aztecs of Mexico, for example, killed and ate all or part of 15,000 sacrificial victims a year.

Nowadays, the only accepted eating of human flesh is in extreme life or death situations, such as the South American soccer team that crashed in the mountains. Stranded, freezing, and starving, they resorted to eating their dead for survival.

In the 1800s, Alfred Parker, stranded in the Colorado Rockies, consumed five members of his party. He was later saved, indicted, and convicted of cannibalism. The judge was particularly annoyed with Parker and condemned him, saying, "There were seven Democrats in Hinsdale County and you've ate five of them, God damn you!" Parker never did hang, but the Democrats never made a strong comeback in the area either.

- Most people would probably choose to die in their sleep, but what about those who kill in their sleep? There have been a number of accounts of somnambulist murders and sleepwalking has actually been recognized as a defense in murder trials in America. But one of the weirdest sleepwalking murders took place in Paris. A police detective named Robert Ledru was investigating the murder of a businessman who had been vacationing in the city. Nearby footprints indicated the murderer had been wearing socks but no shoes during the crime. Ledru also noticed that the murderer had only four toes on one of his feet. Ledru himself was missing a toe and had awakened that morning with damp socks. And his gun was missing two bullets. He checked and discovered that the bullets in the victim had been fired from his own weapon. So, he turned himself in. He was acquitted but ordered to always sleep alone inside a locked room.

- There are those don't wait for the grim reaper, preferring instead to take matters into their own hands. These people just do the deed themselves. Suicide has been on the rise for years. While Denmark is the country with the highest suicide rate, San Francisco can boast of the highest rate for a city.

In ancient China, Egypt, and India a form of suicide called suttee was practiced. When a man died, it was expected that his wife would jump into her husband's funeral pyre so that they could be reunited in the afterlife. Interestingly, only widows practiced suttee. There is no corresponding custom for husbands whose wives die.

Some forms of suicide are considered quite honorable. Harikari, for instance, allowed soldiers to avoid execution by killing themselves. It required the soldier to cut himself with a jeweled dagger and then thrust it into his vital organs. A trusted friend would then behead the guy. Hey . . . what's a friend for?

Many Japanese chose harikari over surrendering at the end of World War II. Kamikazi pilots were also considered suicides of honor. During World War II, over 3,900 pilots chose to die for their cause by flying their bombers directly at their targets and dying a "warrior's death."

Sometimes, suicide comes in groups. In a jungle settlement in Guyana, over 900 followers of Jim Jones, founder and leader of the People's Temple, killed themselves by drinking poison mixed with a Kool Aid-type drink. Jones himself chose not to suffer the indignity and agony of cyanide and instead shot himself and his wife.

The Branch Davidians (an offshoot of the Seventh Day Adventists) got enmeshed in a stand off with the FBI when the Bureau of Alcohol, Tobacco and Firearms staged a raid on the cult's encampment in Texas. The standoff lasted 51 days and ended in fire, explosions, and gunshot wounds (some of which were self-inflicted). Seventy-six people died.

Members of the Solar Temple committed mass suicide by simultaneously detonating bombs in three temple locations—two in Switzerland and one in Canada. Some of the 54 who died were not willing participants.

And in California, 39 members of the Heaven's Gate cult died in the belief that they could hitch a ride on the tail of the Hale-Bopp comet and commence interstellar travel.

↝ In 1970, television newscaster Chris Hubbock announced on a live primetime program, "And now in keeping with Channel 40's policy of always bringing you the latest in blood and guts in living color, you're about to see another first—an attempted suicide." And then she shot herself dead.

↝ The case of Karen Ann Quinlan, a 22-year old from New Jersey who fell into a coma after mixing drugs and alcohol, brought the subject of euthanasia or assisted suicide into the national spotlight. While the family waited for months for the courts to decide whether they had the right to disconnect Karen's respirator, the morality of the issue was hotly debated across the country. Eventually the family was given permission to unhook Quinlan, but they had to move her to another hospital, as the one she was in refused to allow it. She was disconnected and then went on to live for years afterward, although she never came out of the coma. Physician-assistant suicide is legal in some countries, such as Germany and the Netherlands, but not in the United States. Dr. Jack Kevorkian of Michigan is trying to change that and has been arrested numerous times after using his "death machine," which is not unlike lethal injection used for capital punishment except that the patients themselves push a button to start the deadly intravenous.

A KEG PARTY GONE MAD

This bizarre drowning occurred on October 17, 1814 in a small London parish known as St. Giles. Nine people drowned and two homes were destroyed when a wall of beer swept through the tiny neighborhood. St. Giles was a crowded, wretched slum where entire families were packed into single rooms, attics, and cellars. One night a vat containing 3,500 barrels of beer exploded, sending a sea of beer into St. Giles. The poor victims were either swept away, slammed into walls, or buried under debris. Rescuers had to wade in beer up to their waists.

POP QUIZ

QUESTIONS (Answers start on page 125.)

1. The Bubonic Plague of 540 to 590 in Europe has been named by historians as the cause of:

    A. The fall of the Roman Empire.

    B. The beginning of Christianity's stronghold in Europe.

    C. The destruction of the Greek and Roman fields of medicine as they existed.

2. Being struck by lightening and killed is statistically most likely to occur:

    A. While playing baseball or another outdoor sport.

    B. While in the state of Alaska.

    C. While in the state of Florida.

    D. While in the state of confusion.

    E. While marching in the Orange Bowl parade.

3. Malaria has existed since before recorded history and has been associated with many deadly epidemics. Before it was understood that malaria is passed to humans through mosquitos, a lot of people believed it came from:

    A. Having a lower than normal I.Q.

    B. Bad air.

    C. Bad karma.

    D. The moon being angry.

    E. Foot odor.

4. According to the American Medical Association, if you weigh 154 pounds you are likely to die from drinking:

   A. Twelve 8-ounce glasses of clam juice.

   B. 28 alcoholic drinks.

   C. 32 alcoholic drinks.

   D. More than 10 glasses of Cleveland tap water in a four-hour period.

5. In ancient Rome, a person could be executed for:

   A. Stealing water from a well.

   B. Not bowing before the Emperor

   C. Not giving birth to a son.

   D. Singing rude songs.

6. Cholera was the culprit in thousands of deaths. Eventually, people finally figured out it was due to:

   A. An airborne virus.

   B. A bacteria spread through contact with an infected person's sputum.

   C. Drinking infected water.

   D. Hanging out with too many guys named Steve.

7. During the Middle Ages "The Sweats" refered to:

   A. A mysterious fever affecting members of the nobility.

   B. Menopause, for which women could be executed.

   C. The royal fleece clothing.

   D. Tuberculosis, when commoners had it.

8. The state that carries out the highest number of capital punishments is:

   A. California.

   B. New York.

C. Texas.

D. Rhode Island.

9. The Bubonic Plague was known as the Black Death because:

A. Victims coughed up black phlegm.

B. It came from black rats.

C. A man named Joshua Black was the first known victim.

D. It caused dark patches on the skin.

10. World War I soldiers used nature to create an unusual weapon. Which of the following was used?

A. Hot springs.

B. Urine.

C. Ocean water.

D. Mountains.

11. Which of the following is in the most danger of being destroyed by an earthquake?

A. Japan.

B. California.

C. Alaska.

D. Kansas.

12. In Utah and Arkansas, the law says the death penalty can be imposed:

A. Only on people age 21 or older.

B. On children as young as 14.

C. On people caught in possession of narcotics valued at more than $2 million.

D. Only on males.

13. In an effort to make hanging a more effective and humane method of execution, an Irish physician of the 1700s invented:

   A. A higher platform from which to hang the condemned.

   B. A faster trap door.

   C. A new mixture of fibers for nooses.

   D. A new knot.

14. A good hangman was prized for:

   A. His ability to entertain the crowd with rhyming ditties about the accused.

   B. His good looks—he was considered a local celebrity.

   C. His rope, since he was required to supply it.

   D. His ability to subdue frightened and angry victims.

15. In 1910, an avalanche in Washington State cascaded down a mountain taking with it:

   A. A train.

   B. An airplane.

   C. A herd of dairy cattle.

   D. Four politicians.

16. In 1775, more than 50,000 people in Libson died as the result of:

   A. A fire.

   B. An earthquake.

   C. Mad Cow Disease.

   D. Strep throat.

   E. Sleeping with infected prostitutes.

17. Between 1845 and 1852, some 600,000 Irish came to the United States and Canada looking for a better

chance at life. Of the people who remained in Ireland, 1.5 million died. What was culprit?

A. A microbe.

B. A parasite.

C. A fungus.

D. A mold.

E. No Coke, only Pepsi.

18. Which is true about curare?

   A. It is a poison occasionally used as the method of death in English murder mysteries.

   B. It has been used for thousands of years.

   C. It is the active ingredient in the poison-tipped arrows of the Amazon Indians.

   D. It has been used as a relaxant and anesthetic for surgery.

19. Rome wasn't built in a day, but in 64 A.D. most of it burnt in one (or a few, anyway). Nero, the Emperor at the time was not in the city. Why?

   A. He was on vacation.

   B. His soothsayer warned him to leave the city to avoid death.

   C. He was part of a plot to destroy the city.

   D. He was fighting a battle elsewhere.

ANSWERS

1. All three.

   The tiny flea with its even tinier bacteria caused so much sickness, death, and fear that the Roman Empire could not recover. Greek and Roman medicine could do nothing for plague victims, so people lost faith in the science of the times. As a result of this loss of faith, many turned to religion, strengthening the young Christian Church.

2. C. While in the State of Florida.

3. B. Bad air.

   In fact, the word malaria comes from two words that translate to bad air.

4. C. 32 alcoholic drinks.

5. D. Singing rude songs.

6. C. Drinking infected water.

   Cholera was an unpleasant surprise people could get from their drinking water. Outbreaks of cholera were sometimes so severe that bodies would be piled up like cord wood and buried in mass graves.

7. A. A mysterious fever affecting members of the nobility.

   It was a stinking bad time for the British upper class between 1507 and 1517 because a mysterious fever had them sweating and exuding a foul odor. And they said the peasants were revolting! The fever, simply called "the sweats," killed hundreds of English, almost all of them titled and/or monied. The sweats apparently had no affect on the commoners because they had built-in immunities, most likely because of their constant exposure.

8. C. Texas.

   Texas executed 104 criminals between 1977 and 1995. The number of death row inmates far exceeds the number of executions everywhere. The state of Rhode Island doesn't engage in capital punishment.

9. D. It caused dark patches on the skin.

   As the disease progressed, blood vessels would hemmorhage as the system broke down. Random dark patches would appear on the skin, especially under the eyes.

10. D. mountains.

Avalanches in the Italian Alps are so common, that during World War I, soldiers intentionally started avalanches and used them as weapons against the enemy. It is estimated that between 1915 and 1918, some 60,000 men died under the Alps avalanches.

11. A. Japan.

Japan experiences about 1,000 tremors a year because seismic activity is so common along the Japan Trench. According to experts, the Pacific Plate constantly grinding against the Asian Continent may eventually cause a cataclysmic earthquake and a massive tsunami. Although it has roughly the same amount of land mass as California, the Islands of Japan are home to nearly five times as many people. Japan has some of the world's best prediction technology and a nationwide disaster plan.

12. B. On children as young as 14.

Of the 37 states that have legalized the death penalty, nine do not specify a minimum age. Utah and Arkansas specify the youngest age (14), and 11 states use the age of majority (18). The remaining states vary from 15 to 17.

13. A. A higher platform from which to hang the condemned.

It was called "The long drop," and subjected the victim to a 14-foot fall that theoretically would guarantee a clean, quick kill. Unfortunately, it was no more reliable than other methods of hanging. When it was used for two executions in Dublin (both men weighing 160 pounds), one guy's neck broke and he died instantly, but the other fellow's death was a little more guesome. The rope tightened around his neck so quickly it actually decapitated him. It was a little more than the spectators expected.

14. C. His rope, since he was required to supply it.

    Hangmen brought their own ropes to executions. Good rope was hard to come by because it had to be both strong and properly stretched beforehand. Many executions took several tries, most often because the rope would break, or the weight of the victim caused the rope to stretch so much that his feet would touch the ground.

15. A. A train.

    An entire train station, several trains and 100 people plummeted 150 feet into a canyon when tons of snow suddenly avalanched down the Cascade Mountains.

16. B. An earthquake.

17. B. A parasite.

    The Irish Potato Famine was caused by a tiny parasite. A huge portion of Ireland's population starved to death as a result.

18. All four answers are true.

19. A. He was on vacation.

NEXT STOP . . . ?

"Don't let it end like this. Tell them I said something."
—*Last words of Pancho Villa*

WHERE DO WE GO FROM HERE?

No question about death and the afterlife provokes more agony, thought, philosophy, and religious debate. From Buddhists who celebrate death as a way to pass on to their next incarnation, to the Christian realm of heaven . . . to the bizarre Heaven's Gate cult whose members planned to hitchhike their way to the afterworld on the tail end of a comet, everyone appears to have a theory. But, like most of our mysteries of death, we can't be sure of the answer until it happens to us . . . and by then, it's too late. Unless, of course, you hook up with a medium, psychic, or channeler. Then you can tell the family all about it from the great beyond. Or "contact" the authors and we can use your experiences in the next edition of this book.

So after you die, are you going up? Going down? Or are you going somewhere in between . . . the land of the Undead?

HAVE YOU GOT SOUL?

This book is full of autopsy details, body and burial facts . . . but no discussion of death would be complete without exploring the afterworld and the concept of the soul. The problem is that no one knows for sure if the soul really exists. Is there such a separate enitity from the body?

Most world religions have a soul concept. In some, such as Christianity, the soul is propelled to either Heaven or Hell depending on the result of God's judgment. In other religions, such as some Native American traditions, the veil or divide between living and dead isn't as clear-cut. Some Native American stories talk of the soul lingering close to the body after death and of the living sometimes needing to help lost souls find their way to continue their journey.

> Let your soul stand cool and composed before a million universes.
>
> —Walt Whitman

HOW'S YOUR KARMA?

Buddhists believe your karma determines what your next incarnation will be. Therefore the moment of death carries great importance and Buddhists try to face their death without fear or regret—perhaps a universal goal for most of humankind. The soul is bound to a wheel, often depicted in Buddhist or Hindu works of art. This "wheel of life" shows successive deaths, births, and reincarnations.

Buddhist funerals, with chanting, gongs, and incense, precede cremation on a funeral pyre. A celebration meal may follow.

Like the wishing jewel, Nirvana grants all one can desire, brings joy, and sheds light.

—Buddhist scriptures

Though there are numerous Buddhist sects, most Buddhists attempt to achieve nirvana. This would signal an end to the constant spiritual struggle and would signify beoming infinite and unobstructed.

What's Your Sign, Baby?

Just as some of us consult the daily newspaper for our horoscope, Buddhists can have a "death moment" horoscope read. Often, Buddhists have a guru or lama present at their death. The lama helps comfort and guide the dying person as the moment of death draws near, thus ensuring a smoother transition for the soul. Will the soul move on to nirvana or a rebirth? If the lama is present at the precise moment of death, a death horoscope can be drawn up for the family. The death horoscope helps determine the method of the body's disposal and the funeral itself.

DEATH CAN GIVE YOU THE SHIVAS

Most traditional Jews are buried soon after death. Instead of elaborate embalming methods and "viewings," Jews are usually buried more simply—and quickly—with no viewing. Most often, their caskets are not ornate. For seven days after burial, the family sits Shiva. Mirrors in the house are covered and family and

---

EUPHEMISMS

Croak
Pop off
Go to the happy hunting ground
Going home feet first
Join the majority

---

friends bring meals, exchange stories and anecdotes about the dead, and comfort the bereaved.

So where does the Jewish soul go from here? Orthodox Jews believe that when the Messiah comes, faithful Jews will be resurrected from the dead. If not, there's always the Jewish version of hell, called Gehenna.

How Hot Is It?

In Gehenna, the valley of fire, you might be suspended by your eyelids for lustful leers committed on earth. Or perhaps you'll be suspended by your ears if you didn't listen to the Torah. If you gossip while standing around the office water cooler and you later are relegated to hell, plan on being suspended by your tongue. Chains of fire suspending women by the breasts await seductresses. Of course, let's not forget scorpion stings and burning lashes. All in all, not as appealing as a week at Club Med.

Many of those who sleep in the dust of the earth shall awake, some to everlasting life, and some to shame and everlasting contempt.

—Daniel 12:2

WHAT'S IN STORE FOR THOSE WHO BELIEVE IN JESUS?

For Roman Catholics, if there is time and warning, priests will be called to perform Last Rites—now called the "anointing of the sick." Why the change? Because previously, if someone was in the hospital and saw that a priest had been called for Last Rites, the patient sometimes panicked or, more usually, gave up fighting for life. Now, the anointing of the sick may be called for by the seriously ill—not just those for whom death is imminent. So don't panic when you see those black robes coming down the hallway.

Most Roman Catholics are embalmed, dressed in their Sunday best and "laid out" in an open casket for a viewing or wake. The family will usually hold the wake for two or three days, concluding each evening with saying the Rosary or other prayers. During the funeral, the casket (usually closed) is often in the center aisle of the church or up near the altar. A Mass of Christian Burial is said, which usually includes communion for Roman Catholics present at the service. Finally, at the cemetery, the deceased is laid to rest. Often, family or community tradition dictates a luncheon or shared meal afterwards.

Come, I think hell's fable.

—Faustus, in Christopher Marlowe's, *The Tragic History of Dr. Faustus*

Eastern Orthodox funerals are very similar to Roman Catholic services and customs. Sometimes, the night before burial, family members remain with the body all night.

Protestant sects are too numerous to mention, and consequently there is great variety in their traditions. Some denominations discourage open viewing and embalming, preferring instead a closed casket. Some African-American services have open displays of weeping, as well as songs of joy that the person has gone to a better place.

And where do Christian souls go?

Well . . . It all depends on the kind of life you led. Heaven or paradise is awarded to those who have led a good life and earned

Dead paleness Boswell's cheek o'erspread,
His limbs with horror shook;
With trembling haste he left his bed,
and burnt his fatal book.

—Elizabeth Moody, "Dr. Johnson's Book"

a place with God, the Father. Hell is the home of Satan, Lucifer, the Devil—he has many names—and the tormented fallen souls who followed the devil's path in this life.

Of course, there's an exception to every rule and much to the dismay of some of the chaste, there is an exception to this one. Catholics who have led an awful, sinful, despicable life can get a last-minute reprieve from eternal damnation. A true and sincere deathbed conversion will act like a giant eraser and buy a ticket to paradise.

For those who have lived a life of ambiguity—too good to spend the everafter in hell but too sinful for St. Peter to open the gate, Roman Catholics also have a concept of purgatory. If you're not quite ready to enter Heaven and need to make amends, you can spend some time in purgatory to purify yourself, through fire, in order to gain entrance. Of course, if you have a lot of friends still here on earth, they can pray for your soul and hopefully reduce your "sentence" in purgatory.

LET'S MECCA DEAL

Muslims, like Jews, bury their dead simply and quickly. The funeral can be held at home or in the mosque. The dead are buried facing Mecca. Muslins believe in the heaven and hell concept, also based on deeds and piousness in this life. The Koran contains vivid desciptions of both . . . and Hell is a place of eternal torture. So you best behave. However, there

The heaven of each is what each desires.

—Thomas Moore

are different Islamic sects, and most believe that after death all souls stay in a sort of cosmic limbo until the day of resurrection, when souls rejoin their bodies and then proceed to heaven or hell.

> Sweet and sweet is their poisoned note,
> The little snakes of silver throat,
> In mossy skulls that nest and lie,
> Ever singing 'die, oh! die.'
>
> —Thomas Lovell Beddoes, "The Phantom-Wooer"

NEITHER HERE NOR THERE

And what of "lost" souls—those neither destined for Heaven nor Hell, but stuck between here and there? Ghosts, poltergeists, vampires, zombies, and ghouls have long historical traditions that make you wonder. Could there be some other dimension? Some other state of humanity? The Undead?

Hitch a Ride on a Flying Saucer

The Heaven's Gate cult gained national notoriety for trying to hitch a ride on a comet's trail. But they were not the only cult to believe in cosmic immortality through alien life. The Raelian Movement was founded by a race car driver turned "prophet," Rael. Dismissing the idea that humans have souls, Rael preaches that immortaility will come through followers' DNA and a space alien culture. In keeping with this, when followers die, they stipulate that their mortician should cut out a piece of their forehead bone and mail this "third eye" to their leader. Rael claims to give it to his space alien pals. Where are those X-File agents when you need them?

Ghostbusters

Remember your first slumber party? Did you tell ghost stories? The success of the horrorfest series *Friday the 13th* wasn't

Fifteen apparitions have I seen;
The worst a coat upon a coat-hanger.

—W. B. Yeats

because the movies were brilliant film-making. Instead, the movies were just expanded ghost stories—horrible tales we told as kids around the campfire or during the sleepover to scare the heck out of our friends.

However, some say ghosts really exist. Their lore is as old as time itself, it seems. And no one is immune. Ghosts can haunt us ordinary folk or the castles of Great Britain. Windsor Castle is supposely haunted by numerous ghosts, including Queen Elizabeth I and mad King George III.

According to Webster's, a ghost is a disembodied soul that may appear to the living in bodily likeness. Despite being part of the next world, or almost next world, a belief in ghosts is generally not supported by most of the world's major religions. That doesn't stop people from believing in them, of course. Nor does it stop "sightings" in graveyards or "haunted" houses. Here are some of history's more infamous ghosts.

- Lady Howard. Rumored to have poisoned two of her four husbands (you had a 50-50 chance of surviving if you married her), Lady Francis Howard was a legendary beauty from the court of James I. She spent some time in the Tower of London for the murder of Sir Thomas Overbury, but she was later released. After her death, her spirit supposedly haunts Okehampton Castle where she performs a penance each night for the sins she committed on earth.

- The Fox Sisters. In the 1840s, three sisters living near Rochester, New York, claimed they heard rappings and bangings in their house and that the noise kept them awake at night. After investigating, the sisters and their parents claimed the noise was a form of communication from Charles Rosa. Rosa had supposedly been murdered by a previous occupant of the house and his remains were buried in the cellar. Eventually, the sisters decided that the rappings were actually a sort of code that corresponded to the alphabet. They received "messages" from the great beyond from a spirit named Mr. Splitfoot whose real initials were C. R. (a.k.a. the murdered Charles Rosa). They took their skills as "mediums" on the road, becoming a stage act. In the 1890s, after the Fox sisters died, human remains were actually found in their cellar verifying that something was indeed afoot. But whether it was Mr. Splitfoot was never determined.

- Abraham Lincoln. Ol' Honest Abe may actually haunt the White House. According to legend, Calvin Coolidge's wife saw the figure of Abraham Lincoln staring out the window of the Oval Office. Others reported hearing Lincoln's ghostly footsteps in various parts of the White House. Later, Queen Wilhelmina of the Netherlands, and a believer in spirits, thought she saw Abraham Lincoln in the hall. The next day she reported this to Franklin D. Roosevelt, who admitted that she was staying in the Lincoln bedroom. One of Roosevelt's secretaries also reported a sighting of Lincoln, and one of the president's dogs took to behaving strangely at times and barking for no reason (some say this was evidence of a "ghost").

- Jeremy Bentham. A founding Utilitarian and philosopher, Bentham believed that the dead should not be interred underground. Rather, he proposed that they be stuffed and set on display as a source of "inspiration." (What sort of inspiration a corpse could provide is unsure, but Bentham was known as an eccentric.) When he died, he stipulated his corpse be embalmed and put in a glass case at the University of London. Eventually, his mummified head began to fall apart and was replaced with a wax head. Perhaps this upset the spirit of Bentham, because he is rumored to haunt the University.

- The Brown Lady of Raynham Hall. This ghost, oh-so-imaginatively named because she wears a brown dress, theoretically haunts Raynham Hall in Norfolk, England. Actually "photographed" by two magazine photographers from *Country Life*, she reputedly wears a brown satin dress and has no eyes—only ghastly sockets where her eyes *should* be. The photograph is a shot of a staircase with a wispy figure floating in the middle of it. Taken in 1936, the photo could be a fraud, though it has never been proven so. It could also be the result of a camera or film flaw, but given that so many people had previously reported seeing the Brown Lady, perhaps these two photographers actually caught her on film.

- Carl Jung believed we could, through telepathy, talk with the deceased. In his autobiography, he wrote of an experience in which he had a vision following the funeral of a friend. In the vision, his friend brought him to his (the deceased's) library and wanted Jung to pay attention to a specific book on the shelf whose title Jung could not see. The next day, Jung went to his friend's widow's house and found the exact volume his friend had been pointing out in the vision—Emile Zola's *The Legacy of Death*.

- In southern Italy in 1939, a young girl named Maria appeared to become possessed by the spirit or ghost of a young man named Pepe Veraldi. She had never known Pepe, who had drowned three years previously, but she took on his mannerisms and voice and called people around her by the names of the dead man's friends.

Then, in Pepe's voice, she told of being murdered—but the murderers had made it appear to be a suicide. Perhaps compelled by the ghost or spirit, she jumped from a bridge and lapsed into a coma until Pepe's mother approached Maria and commanded the spirit to leave, which it appeared he did. Maria opened her eyes and returned to normal. Later, one of the murderer's confessed—and the murder, he said, had been carried out in the precise manner Maria had described while possessed by the spirit.

- Old Jeffrey. John Wesley, the founder of the Methodist church, had a boyhood home, a haunted rectory in England, that was supposedly inhabited by a poltergeist. He and his siblings called the poltergeist "Old Jeffrey" and they often played games with this mischievious spirit who knocked and made noises, pushed people, played with latches and dishes, and otherwise made his presence very known.

- Malicious poltergeists apparently strangled a daughter and harmed a son of an 1800s Presbyterian minister. According to the tale, the minister was visited by no fewer than 30 poltergeist figures who often threw things, broke glasses, and delivered ghostly messages. A curiosity, the minister observed these activities for over a year—but then the poltergeists turned ugly and harmed two of his children before vanishing as mysteriously as they arrived.

A Farewell Appearance

At, or shortly after, the moment of death, crisis apparitions can appear to friends and loved ones to help them deal with and accept the loss, to deliver a last word or message, or to tell loved

The soul unfolds itself, like a lotus of countless petals.

—Kahlil Gibran

ones to move on. The phenomenon is widely reported across all age groups, races, and cultures. Of course, psychologists will explain the apparition as a way for the traumatized mind and psyche of the bereaved to process the death. But people who have seen one of these "ghosts" will swear that they were of sound mind, not dreaming, and that the ghost was "quite real."

Collect Call from Late Aunt Sylvia

In perhaps another form of crisis apparition, Thomas Edison, whose parents were spiritualists, allegedly believed communication was possible between this world and the next. He even tried to build a telephone that would allow the earth-bound to speak with their dearly departed.

Though Edison never successfully invented a phone that will let us call our late Aunt Sylvia, there are people who believe they've had phone calls with the dead. Sometimes these calls consist of a person calling "from beyond the grave" with a very fuzzy phone connection. They usually call to say good-bye or sometimes to deliver an urgent message. Occasionally, a phone call from the dead consists of calling Aunt Sylvia and talking with her—only to find out later that she died earlier that day . . . so just who—or what—were you talking to?

Get Out Your High Heels and Garlic Necklace

Most of us have seen at least one old Dracula film. Even Abbott and Costello met a vampire. In the old movies, Dracula wore a black cape and put women in flimsy nightgowns into a trance before biting them on the neck and sucking their blood.

These Draculas weren't particularly good-looking. But then along came the young Frank Langella in *Dracula*. More recently, the sexy triumverate of Tom Cruise, Brad Pitt, and Antonio Banderas in *Interview with the Vampire* brought the modern-day celluloid vampire into the realm of sex, sex, sex. Some literary critics have even commented on the phallic nature of Dracula's long teeth. So the legend has entwined with both sex and immortality.

> He throws no shadow; he can make in the mirror no reflect... He can be as a bat... He can come in the mist which he create . . . He can see in the dark—no small power this . . .
>
> —Bram Stoker, *Dracula*

But did you know that there are distinct varieties of vampires? Many cultures, besides Transylvanian legend, have vampires. Sometimes they drink blood, have an aversion to garlic, and can't see their reflections in the mirror. But other vampires are the souls of unbaptized babies. There are vampires who are part vampire, part magician; vampires who like to drink sheep's blood; and vampires who are female. In modern times, the vampire has been depicted on film and in books as a serial killer, lesbian, and feminist.

How can someone become a vampire? Vampirism can be inherited. You can be bitten by a vampire and thus become one.

EUPHEMISMS

Join the invisible choir
Launch into eternity
Swimming in the River Styx
Done pumping blood
Pay the debt of nature

Both life and death are part of the same great adventure.

—Theodore Roosevelt

However, other factors have been associated with this lore including committing suicide, having sex with your grandma, being born on Christmas day (presumably because your mother dared to give birth to you on a day dedicated to the Virgin Mary and Christ), working on Sundays, smoking on a holy day, and drinking excessively (given these last three, there are likely many more vampires than the world realizes).

Not the Drink, Silly

Zombies are dead people. Sort of. According to legend, zombies are dead people brought back to life—without their soul. They eat nothing, work tirelessly for no pay, needing no rest, and follow the every command of their sorcerer-masters. Sounds like they need a union.

Zombies do supposedly exist in Haiti. According to Wade Davis, who published an account in 1985 called *The Serpent and the Rainbow* of his personal experiences with voodoo society, zombies are people who have been psychologically tortured by voodoo sorcerers. Tetrodotoxin is a poison derived from the skin of two species of puffer fish, that applied to the skin produces a death-like state. According to Davis (and others), voodoo sorcerers make zombie slaves out of the poor and disenfrachised using tetrodotoxin. Victims first feel weak and dizzy, begin to sweat and suffer from headaches. After causing violent bouts of diarrhea and vomiting, the poison then attacks the nervous system. Twitching, paralysis, and finally a death-

Last words of English writer Joseph Addison:

"See in what peace a Christian can die."

like coma follow. Victims are buried alive so that, Davis theorizes, the voodoo sorcerer can retrieve the body and administer the antidote to the pufferfish posion. The person is, naturally, scared out of his or her mind, disoriented and still weak. Frequently abused by the sorcerer, the victim's psychological torture is soon complete. The sorcerer "re-names" the person and declares the "zombie" is now the sorcerer's slave.

POP QUIZ

QUESTIONS (Answers start on page 147.)

1. How many circles of torment existed in the hell of Dante's Divine Comedy?
   A. 1
   B. 3
   C. 9
   D. Infinite

2. Limbo, part of the Roman Catholic tradition prior to Vatican II, was a place where:
   A. Souls got to enjoy themselves at an everlasting party, hence the "limbo" dance popular in Carribean culture.
   B. The soul essentially "fills out forms," waiting to be called for judgment.
   C. Unbaptized babies can stay until they are admitted to heaven through the prayers of the faithful still on earth.
   D. Lucifer questions the soul to see if you are a candidate for Hell.

3. True or False? Orthodox Jews support cremation as a form of atonement for earthly sins.

4. In Buddhist traditions, "transmigration" refers to:
   A. The migration of an entire family to escape religious persecution.

B. An exit visa.

C. The migration of part of the essence of a person into another human or animal body.

D. Buddha's original life journey.

5. In the Middle Ages, bodies could be ejected from cemeteries if:

A. The person had died from The Black Plague.

B. The dead person was believed to be a vampire.

C. The dead person's family could not pay a "burial tax."

D. The dead person committed suicide.

6. Practitioners of necromancy:

A. Are in love with a dead person.

B. Believe the living can make direct contact with the dead.

C. Make love to a dead body.

D. Summon Satan in order to raise a person from the dead.

7. A "ghoul" is:

A. A spirit who haunts once a year on Halloween.

B. The highest level of "ghost."

C. The headless spirit of a person killed during the French Revolution.

D. A monster that haunts cemeteries and feeds on dead bodies.

8. Count Dracula, the "hero" of Bram Stoker's famous book, is said to be based on an actual prince. According to legend, Vlad the Impaler:

A. Took the blood and flesh of his victims and fed it to his prized collection of bats.

B. Liked to impale his enemies on poles.

   C. Had an aversion to garlic.

   D. Had dentures specially made to puncture victims that he bit in the heat of battle.

9. In Ireland, if a "banshee" stops outside your house:

   A. It is time to end your period of mourning.

   B. Someone in your house will die within 24 hours.

   C. You are going to hell.

   D. You must invite the banshee in for a pint of ale.

10. Vampires are known to change their shape. Bats are a common transformation. Which of these other transformations is *not* attributed to vampires?

   A. Raven.

   B. Cockroach.

   C. Spider.

   D. Wolf.

11. While they are immortal, vampires can be killed by driving a stake through their heart. If this makes you squeamish, you can choose a number of other methods. However, which of the following ways will *not* kill a vampire:

   A. Beheading with a gravedigger's shovel.

   B. Exorcism.

   C. Exposing the vampire to daylight.

   D. Burning the body.

12. What is a psychopomp?

   A. A cross-dressing serial killer.

   B. A psychotic vampire.

   C. A divine guide who leads lost souls to the land of the dead.

D. Someone who claims to channel spirits but is ex-
    posed as a fraud.

13. What is Tibetan yoga of the dead?

A. Tibetan yoga of the dead? It's what one of the authors
    wishes on her yoga teacher after a particularly gruel-
    ing workout.

B. It is yoga performed by dead spirits in the afterworld.

C. It is a meditation form to guide the spirit on its
    afterlife journey.

D. It is a particular yoga position meant to resemble a
    corpse.

ANSWERS

1. C. 9

2. C. Unbaptized babies can stay until they are admitted to
    heaven through the prayers of the faithful still on earth.

    In some parishes, prior to Limbo's fading in Roman
    Catholic teachings, schoolchildren even raised money
    for the Limbo Babies in order to help them pass to
    heaven.

3. False. Othodox Jews believe cremation will interfere with
    a bodily resurrection.

4. C. The migration of part of the essence of a person into
    another human or animal body.

5. D. The dead person committed suicide.

6. B. Believe the living can make direct contact with the
    dead.

    Necromancy is an ancient tradition. In Greek mythology,
    Odysseus visited Hades to consult with the dead.

7. D. Monster that haunts cemeteries and feeds on dead bodies.

8. B. Liked to impale his enemies on poles.

9. B. Someone in your house will die within 24 hours.

   A banshee, sometimes riding in a death coach, signifies someone in a house dying the next day. The coach, usually noted by its headless driver and black horses, is the equivalent of the grim reaper.

10. B. Cockroach.

11. B. Exorcism.

    Sorry, wrong movie.

12. C. A divine guide who leads lost souls to the land of the dead.

13. C. It is a meditation form to guide the spirit on its afterlife journey (much as one of the authors wishes it were "A.")

Hell No, We Won't Go

"All my possessions for a moment of time."

Last words of Elizabeth I

The end is inevitable, but the will to survive has occasionally proven stronger than the forces of fate. In situations where death seems inescapable, there are people who have fought their way back from atrocious injuries, performed acts of superhuman strength, or even resorted to cannibalism in the hopes of living to see another day. There are also documented cases of "miracle cures," in which people with fatal illnesses have regained their health using nontraditional methods.

One such case is Norman Cousins, an American who eventually wrote a book detailing his experience. He was diagnosed with an incurable disease in 1964. In great pain and unable to

Last words of
Lady Astor, when she woke briefly during her last illness and found all her family around her bedside:

"Am I dying or is this my birthday?"

move his arms and legs, Cousins set out to heal himself using laughter as medicine. He filled his days with humor—listening, reading, and watching anything with a punchline. Much to the amazement of his doctors, he laughed himself right out of his sick bed and was well enough to return to work within a few months.

Sometimes, postponing one's death can be a case of mind over matter. Thomas Jefferson and John Adams were both fast approaching the pearly gates in 1826, but completely unaware of what the other was doing, each managed to delay his respective appointment with St. Peter. Prior to becoming gravely ill, they had promised one another they would live to see the 50th anniversary of the signing of the Declaration of Independence. On the Fourth of July their goal was accomplished, their willpower was expended, and each died before the end of the day.

And then there is the case of Shigechiyo Izumi of Japan, who simply wasn't planning on going—at least not until he was good and ready. He was born on June 29, 1865, and is listed as a young boy in Japan's first census, taken in 1871. When he was 70 he

"For three days after death your hair and fingernails continue to grow, but phone calls taper off."

—Johnny Carson

started drinking a glass of rum each day, which he later credited to his longevity. After a couple of lifetimes of smoking, he gave up the habit when he was 116. He finally died on February 21, 1986 at the ripe old age of 120.

Some folks, however, seem to escape the clutches of the Grim Reaper through nothing more than

෴

> ## EUPHEMISMS
>
> Become worm food
> Become crow bait
> Feed the vultures
> Gone to the great beyond
> Answer the final summons
>
> ෴

sheer luck. You can call it a twist of fate or say it just wasn't their time, but while the following people were staring death in the face, it was death that blinked first.

ANSWERING TO A HIGHER AUTHORITY?

Of course you may think it was a sign from above, rather than luck, that saved Gabriel Magalhaens. While working in China as a missionary, he was arrested and sentenced to death on six different occasions. But the night before each of the scheduled executions, he was able to escape because earthquakes damaged his prison. When he finally did die, it was of natural causes.

An even stranger story of survival took place in 1902. Mt. Pelee in the West Indies erupted and all 30,000 inhabitants of St. Pierre were all killed within a few minutes. All except one, that is. Raoul Sarteret, a convicted murderer, survived in his jail cell. Eventually, he was pardoned and went on to become a missionary.

For John Lee, eluding death was a matter of technical difficulty. He was scheduled for execution on February 23, 1885. After three attempts to hang him failed because the trap door wouldn't open (and officials were unable to determine why— each time the door failed Lee was removed, the door was tried and it worked), his sentence was commuted to life. He was paroled in 1907 and died of natural causes four years later.

Australian Joseph Samuels was saved by bad hemp. Officials tried to hang him three times in 1803. Each time, he escaped death because the rope broke, so they gave up and set him free.

In Scotland, Margaret Dixon, who was convicted of murder, had been hanging for an hour when her husband came to collect her body for burial. But on the way to the cemetery she revived, so he brought her home instead. She lived 25 more years.

And in 1705 an Englishman named John Smith recovered after he went to the gallows. For the rest of his life, he was known as Half-hung Smith.

> "I am ready to meet my maker but whether my maker is prepared for the great ordeal of meeting me is another matter."
>
> —Deepak Chopra

Forget luck, Mother Nature or technical problems, in Medieval England a criminal could escape the death penalty with a good memory. Although capital punishment was considered reasonable for a myriad of behaviors, it was only given in secular court. Within the church, there was no death sentence. So if a defendant could prove a connection with the clergy, he could be tried in ecclesiastical court. Since almost all the educated people were members of the clergy, it stood to reason that if a person could read they were a cleric. The test of literacy was to read the first verse of Psalm 51, which became known as the "neck verse." Savvy law breakers usually took the time to memorize it.

MAYBE I'LL TAKE THE 4:15 INSTEAD

Next time you are delayed by some irritating inconvenience, consider this:

Edmund Hillary, the first person to reach the top of Mt. Everest, missed a United flight because he was late to the airport. The plane collided in mid-air with a TWA flight, killing 134 people.

Elizabeth Taylor also missed a fatal flight when she was unable to travel because she came down with the flu.

Vladmir Zworkykin, who is known as the father of modern television, was planning to return to New York on the S.S.Athenia. But when he realized he forgot his tuxedo, he was too embarrassed to go aboard without proper dinner attire. Lucky for him, he took a later ship. The S.S. Athenia was torpedoed by the Nazis.

Novelist Jerzy Kozinski was on his way to Sharon Tate's house on the fatal night Charles Manson's followers showed up. But an airline had lost Kozinski's luggage, delaying him and saving his life.

And gangster Bugs Moran wasn't a victim of the St. Valentine's Day Massacre because, although he was supposed to be there, he arrived late. Afterwards, he said he was delayed because he "had a really busy day."

Last words of Robert Drew, executed on August 2, 1994:

"Remember, the death penalty is murder."

HUGH ARE SO LUCKY!

A man named Hugh Williams was the only survivor when his boat sank in the Irish Sea in 1664. So, okay, that could happen. But then in 1785, another, entirely different Hugh Williams was the lone survivor of a ship that also went down in the Irish Sea. What a coincidence. In 1820, yet another boat sunk and guess the name of sole survivor? You've got it —Hugh Williams.

Last words of Nicolas-Sebastien Chamfort, French writer, suicide note:

"And so I leave this world, where the heart must either break or turn to lead."

PAYING ATTENTION IN SCHOOL REALLY DOES MATTER

Joseph Spah was riding in the Hindenburg when it exploded into flames, but his training as a professional acrobat came in handy when he climbed out and hung there for a moment calculating his jump. He fell 50 feet, went into a roll and escaped.

JUST PLAIN WEIRD

Sometimes things defy explanation.

- In Hammond, Indiana, a 24-foot length of steel rod shot through Paul Koviski's skull and became lodged there. It entered his neck and exited over his right eye. To the attending doctors' amazement, he not only survived, he suffered no ill effects.

- Death, or at least dismemberment, by a runaway engine seemed a sure thing when Jerry Simpson looked up from his work on a bridge and saw a train bearing down on him. Since the Cascade Mountain bridge was suspended over a deep gully there wasn't anywhere for Jerry to go. With only a moment to think, he made the decision to make his death certain and instantaneous and threw himself directly into the train's path. Imagine his surprise when he looked up to see the North Pacific engine derail and plunge into the ravine at the last moment.

- In the late-1890's, a tornado apparently swept up a baby and deposited him in a treetop on a farm in Missouri. When the farmer who lived there went out to survey the tornado damage, he found the baby. The infant boy was in perfect health. No one was ever able to identify the baby, so the farmer ended up raising him.

- Frank Tower was on the Titanic and was one of the survivors. One year later, he was sailing on the Empress of Ireland when it sunk. Again, he arrived home safely. A year after that, wouldn't you know, he swam away from the Lusitania when it went down. And they called Molly Brown unsinkable. Of course, we wouldn't recommend going on a cruise with this guy.

- In 1669, an entire seaside village slid into the sea. Despite the fact that Runswick, England disappeared very quickly, there was not a single injury. The reason? Everyone who lived there was attending a funeral in a neighboring town at the time. The were probably surprised when they went home, though.

- Although he tried to commit suicide by jumping off the Empire State Building, John Helms landed on a ledge on the 85th floor and survived.

- It could have been an incredible disaster when a B-25 flown from Massachusetts to Newark, New Jersey took a detour—right into the Empire State Building. The plane smashed into the building between the 78th and 79th floors, where it got stuck. The engines broke loose and one sliced through an elevator cable, causing the elevator to plummet 80 floors, and the other went through the building, crashing through the opposite side. On a normal day, such an accident would have claimed hundreds and hundreds of lives. But because the building was nearly empty at the time there were only 13 casualties, three of them people who were on the plane.

- The Great Chicago Fire was reputedly started when Mrs. O'Leary's cow knocked over a kerosene lamp. Although the fire caused $400 million in damage and 500 people were dead or missing, the cow was fine.

HEY, I AIN'T DEAD YET!

Daniel Boone, Wild Bill Hickock, P.T. Barnum and Bertrand Russell all read their own obituaries. So did Mark Twain, who responded by saying, "Reports of my death are greatly exaggerated." Reading about your own death would probably affect anyone; for Alfred Nobel, the affect was profound. He was extremely distressed when he came across an erroneous notice of his death. As the inventor of dynamite, his obituary referred to him as a "merchant of death." He was so upset by this perception that it was one of the reasons he established the Nobel Prize for those who do the most to advance peace, literature, and the sciences.

BIBLIOGRAPHY

Andreu, Guillemette. *Egypt in the Age of the Pyramids*. Ithaca, NY: Cornell University Press, 1997.

Arnold, Larry E. *Ablaze! The Mysterious Fires of Spontaneous Human Combustion*. NY: M. Evans and Company, Inc., 1995.

Brandreth, Gyles. *Famous Last Words & Tombstone Humor*. NY: Sterling Publishing Co., Inc., 1989.

Cohen, Daniel. *The Encyclopedia of Ghosts*. NY: Dodd, Mead & Company, 1984.

Donaldson, Norman. *How Did They Die?* NY: St. Martin's Press, 1981.

Enright, D. J. *The Oxford Book of the Supernatural*. Oxford: Oxford University Press, 1994.

Fast, Julius & Fast, Timothy. *The Legal Atlas of the United States.* NY: Facts on File, Inc., 1997.

Gonzálaz-Wippler. *The Complete Book of Spells, Ceremonies & Magic.* St. Paul: Llewellyn Publications, 1996.

Herbst, Judith. *Bio Amazing: A Casebook of Unsolved Human Mysteries.* NY: Atheneum, 1985.

Jones, Constance. *R.I.P. The Complete Book of Death & Dying.* NY: Harper Collins Publishers (Stonesong Press), 1997.

Kindersley, Dorling Ltd. (ed.). *Reader's Digest Facts & Fallacies Stories of the Strange and Unusual.* Reader's Digest Association; Pleasantville, New York; 1988.

Lewis, James R. *Encyclopedia of Afterlife Beliefs and Phenomena.* Detroit: Gale Research, Inc., 1994.

Miller, David. *Ripley's Believe It or Not! Accidents & Disasters Marvels of Nature.* NY: Coward, McCann & Geoghegan, 1982.

Morris, Desmond. *The Human Animal: A Personal View of the Human Species.* NY: Crown Publishers, 1994.

The New Encyclopaedia Britannica (15th ed). Chicago: Encyclopaedia Britannica, Inc.

Panati, Charles. *Panati's Extraordinary Endings of Practically Everything and Everybody.* NY: Harper & Row Publishers, 1989.

Randi, James. *An Encyclopedia of Claims, Frauds, and Hoaxes of the Occult and Supernatural.* NY: St. Martin's Press, 1995.

Ripley's Believe It or Not! Book of Chance. NY: Coward, McCann & Geoghegan, Inc., 1982.

Wallace, Irving, Wallechinsky, David, Wallace, Amy, Wallace, Sylvia. *The People's Almanac Presents The Book of Lists #2.* NY: William Morrow and Company, Inc., 1980.

Wallace, Amy, Wallechinsky, David, and Wallace, Irving. *The People's Almanac Presents The Book of Lists #3*. NY: William Morrow and Company, Inc., 1983.

Walker, Bryce. *Earthquake*. Alexandria VA: Time-Life Books, 1987.

Whitfield, Barbara Harris, *Spiritual Awakenings*. Deerfield Beach, FL: Health Communications, Inc., 1995.

INDEX

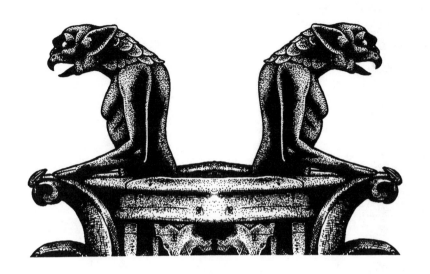

ABOUT THE AUTHORS

Erica Orloff and JoAnn Baker are both freelance writers. Orloff, who lives in Florida, has published numerous articles, children's stories, and fiction pieces. In addition, she has her own editorial consulting business and works with publishers and authors from around the country. A book editor since the mid-1980s, she has worked on hundreds of books, many of which have been bestsellers.

Baker, who lives in New York, works as a journalist and writes a weekly humor column. She is the author of *The View From My House,* a collection of humorous essays.

Orloff and Baker have known each other for more than a decade and during that time have developed a deep and abiding respect for one another, not for their professional accomplishments, but rather for the offbeat way each of them looks at and deals with the world.

Saturn Press

Order These Other Exciting Titles From Saturn Press

Saturn Press • 17639 Foxborough Lane • Boca Raton FL 33496
www.saturnpress.com • email: *drlevinson@saturnpress.com*

Saturn Press

Order These Other Exciting Titles From Saturn Press

1-88584309-7 • $12.95(p) Sept

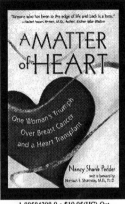

1-88584308-9 • $19.95(HC) Oct

THE BIG SLEEP:
True Tales & Twisted Trivia
about Death
Erica Orloff
JoAnn Baker

Here's a book that will both intrigue and fascinate you. It contains facts you wouldn't know, stories you couldn't know, and accounts you shouldn't know.

A MATTER OF HEART:
One Woman's Triumph Over
Breast Cancer and a Heart
Transplant
Nancy Pedder

A beautifully told story of one woman's determination to survive both breast cancer and a heart transplant. Underscores the priceless gift of organ donation.

Saturn Press • 17639 Foxborough Lane • Boca Raton FL 33496
www.saturnpress.com • email: *drlevinson@saturnpress.com*